Voice

IN THE AMERICAN WEST

ANDY WILKINSON, SERIES EDITOR

ALSO IN THIS SERIES:

Bad Smoke, Good Smoke: A Rancher's View of Texas Wildfire
by John R. Erickson

Cowboy's Lament: A Life on the Open Range
by Frank Maynard; edited by Jim Hoy

Gypsy Alibi: A Gonzo Memoir
by Bob Livingston

The Hell-Bound Train: A Cowboy Songbook, Second Edition
by Glenn Ohrlin; edited by Charlie Seemann

If I Was a Highway
by Michael Ventura

In My Father's House: A Memoir of Polygamy
by Dorothy Allred Solomon

Llano Estacado: An Island in the Sky
edited by Stephen Bogener and William Tydeman

Light in the Trees
by Gail Folkins

On Becoming Apache
by Harry Mithlo and Conger Beasley Jr.

Ordinary Skin: Essays from Willow Springs
by Amy Hale Auker

Rightful Place
by Amy Hale Auker

Small Town Author
by John R. Erickson

A Sweet Separate Intimacy: Women Writers of the American Frontier, 1800–1922
edited by Susan Cummins Miller

Texas Dance Halls: A Two-Step Circuit
by Gail Folkins and J. Marcus Weekley

Texas Red
by Red Steagall, with Jim Jennings

Other books by Amy M. Hale (as Amy Hale Auker)

Livestock Man
Ordinary Skin: Essays from Willow Springs
Rightful Place
The Story Is the Thing
Winter of Beauty

DRINKING WILD WATER

Essays

Amy M. Hale

TEXAS TECH UNIVERSITY PRESS

This book is typeset in Adobe Caslon Pro. The paper used in this book meets the minimum requirements of ANSI/NISO Z39.48-1992 (R1997). ∞

Designed by Hannah Gaskamp
Cover design by Hannah Gaskamp
Cover photo by author
Frontspiece by Kat Richards

Library of Congress Cataloging-in-Publication Data on file

ISBN: 978-1-68283-276-9 (paperback)
ISBN: 978-1-68283-277-6 (ebook)

Texas Tech University Press
Box 41037
Lubbock, Texas 79409-1037 USA
800.832.4042
ttup@ttu.edu
www.ttupress.org

Dedicated to P!NK, who taught me to say, "I am here."
And to Bullwinkle, my carrier of light.
And to the circle of sisters who sit around the fire with me . . .
you'll find me on the smoky side.

Some authors preface their works by stating that the names of people have been changed to protect privacy, that most valuable of commodities. I open by noting that the names of locations have been changed to protect the almost untouched and sacred places I went to write these words. I changed them to protect the wild, for the wild does not protect itself but invites us in . . . until she kicks us back out.

AMH

CONTENTS

SWEETLY SINGING

The alarm sings at 4 a.m.
Ours is a work song—
         a song of doing, with hands and hearts—
                  a heartbeat song.
It is an I-N-G song—
         a song of rising, going, growing,
                  moving, mounting, being there
where the work is always waiting.
Ours is a living song,
         a defining song, a refining song—
                  trial by fire—
a some days are hard in 4/4 time song.
It is a cycle song, a season song,
a never-ending circle song—
                  with weather. And death.
Ours is a sweet singing,
a lowing, a keening, a coyote howling in the canyon,
         a falling rain and deepgurgle creek song.
We always sing of water.

Ours is a song of fire and wind,
         wood and plants,
stone and that ancient dance—
a song of trying again
                  and love

and lists.
Don't forget to stop at the feed store.
Ours is a walking song—
    allegretto upon the trail,
      a single-file dust song—
a bawling for babies melody—
    bass notes of bellowing bull telling the whole world we
are on our way.
Yes, sweetly singing, we are on our way.

(Originally published in *Livestock Man*, Pen-L Publishing, 2018. The author can be heard reciting this poem in *The New York Times* online video essay entitled "Work Songs of the Cowboy Poets," March 9, 2019.)

DRINKING WILD WATER

INTRODUCTION: WORK SONG

The best introduction to a book I have ever read is Clarissa Pinkola Estés's opening in *Women Who Run with the Wolves*. The best intro track on an album is the lead-off for Andy Wilkinson's *Radio Free America*, a collection of poems and songs, starting with "Something to Say," and, indeed, he does have. The best first poem in a collection is "The Pasture" by Robert Frost, an invitation to join him in his agrarian life.

While I won't pretend that I can write an introduction as powerful as Estés's or compose a song as crystal clear as Wilkinson's, I do extend an invitation.

In 2006 I finished writing a manuscript called *Rightful Place*, a love letter to lifestyle and sense of place. The book wasn't published until 2011 because of a series of bureaucratic complications and my fear of being labeled a prima donna for speaking up in defense of my work that had been forgotten in the pile once again. *Rightful Place* won awards. It was lifted by strong, confident women who are not threatened by sister voices.

And I learned to sing. With ink, on the page.

Since I began writing that book, my life has shifted and changed, been sundered by divorce and stitched back together with love. The woman who wrote those essays was a homeschooling mom living

3

on ranch camps at the ends of long dirt roads on commercial cattle operations. She cooked for cowboy crews and heard the breaking news of 9/11 over an FM radio station, not quite sure what the Twin Towers even were, having grown up in a very sheltered home with no television. That woman graduated from high school in a county where, in 2016, Hillary Clinton got a total of six votes, and wrote from a culture where churchgoing parents were challenged to decide *what to do about Harry Potter*. That woman evolved through the years into one who still lives at the end of a long dirt road but who deeply regrets not having marched in a sisterhood sea of pink hats. My guy often asks, "How did you get from there to here?" and he doesn't mean from Texas to Arizona.

My children grown and flown, I now earn my paycheck as a cowboy on a ranch that includes a United States Forest Service (USFS) grazing allotment. I've evolved from a woman who walked for miles and miles on the wind-scoured prairie to an avid backpacker in these mountains scored by deep veins of rock and water. I blame Ed Abbey. Dude, I've crawled on my knees across the sandstone in your honor.

I have written other books, won other awards, fought for my work, and learned to be at home in this world.

Like the dragonfly larvae that live in the mud of the creek bottoms, I molt over and over. I shed tired crackly dry skin for fresh tender new skin, and have come to embrace and love the process, recognizing the rightfulness even when it itches. But one thing hasn't changed. Washed up on the shores of this strange wonderful horrible time, this time of examination and caution and shifting sands, I find that I am, once again, writing love letters . . . to the universe, to individuals, to the land, to change, to work, and even, at times, to who I am becoming beneath my skin.

In these troubled and uncertain times, I think, almost daily, of Toni Morrison reminding us that now, without self-pity or fear, is when the artists go to work. So I pick up my pen and fail. Pick it up again and fail again. But I continue to pick it up, even after I have thrown it across the room, writing my way through the noise and discord and confusion, through the messiness that is life. Morrison also said that a writer must write the book we ourselves want to read, and in some ways, this is it . . . a book that says come along with me to this really cool place where I live and work and it probably looks nothing like where you live and work but we may find out that we are more alike than we are different, that we have similar wounds that need healing, similar joys and griefs, similar dreams even as our modes of locomotion through life and daily scenery differ. I believe in the power of story to unify and heal.

In the words of the old farmer poet, "Won't you come, too?" I invite you into the space where we find more questions than answers and sometimes the best thing we can do is sit in a camp chair by the fire and talk about each cow we gathered. Or take off our shoes, put our feet in the creek, and have a snack. Or rise early and try to make sense of things before the dawn, listening for that old elk slow-stepping in the creek bottom and blending his lonely song with that of the sleepy owl.

The ranch where I live and work is a big place, fifty-thousand acres in all. The official description with location would say Arizona, high desert, piñon juniper interface, *mal pais* mesas, elevation from over six thousand feet above sea level to down around three, pine trees to chaparral to low Sonoran Desert. At its heart, its heartbeat, is ranch headquarters, an island of eight hundred acres of patented land with sub-irrigated bottoms, granite boulders piled high, a big pond with a yellow canoe and cattails, and a cluster of houses and barns, hugged on all sides by national forest. Private land butted up against public, maps and management overseen by government agencies, grazing lease signed in offices by men who don't live or ride out here. My husband, Gail, and I don't own one horse or one cow, but we have a lot of horses and a lot of cows. We work for wages.

That is the official description, but my description has a different, more personal, melody. I sing of bears who live in the pine trees on the upper end, but of a day with two bear sightings down in the low country when the prickly pear tunas were bright shining red and every pile of scat was laden with seeds. Of Gila monsters and mountain lions and how one time I saw a sidewinder, as white as the alkaline dirt, and how I thought it was an albino until I did some research. I would tell of monsoon season when it must get blistering hot so that it will rain every afternoon around two o'clock. I would tell of an Arizona that is not Phoenix and of two growing periods in the year, at least when the summer moisture comes, autumns full of springtime wildflowers. I would tell of heavy wet snowfall and feeding the birds in this migratory corridor and species variation from soft gentle fleeting mosses and ferns to ancient arm-raised saguaro cactus. I would tell of glow time, those magic moments in the evenings when the sky and the rocks are touched by every fire color imaginable.

I would point north and west and tell of a deep canyon that runs south, filled with bright white granite boulders, blue-black permanent pools, barriers, and black hawks. I'd point west, with a little southern angle, and tell of how that canyon runs into another watershed, the one that starts here where we stand, here where we can see heirloom apple and pear trees planted in the creek bottom by long-ago homesteaders, and how the rainfall runs off chattering in the rocks and sand and becomes a waterfall many miles away, one that holds a muddy bear track and my heart.

This ranch, these seventy-two square miles, is where I have found me. The past me—tender and naïve and unwise. The present me—initiated and determined and seasoned; the wildish me with the crust of dried-up domestication around the edges. The future me—agèd and old, wrinkled and wise and tired and timeless and worn. This ranch has ancient bones and veins and skin and voice, singular and collective, a blend of solitary songs and calls strung together with the motion of the planet, so loud that the sun and moon, stationary orbs, seem to move across the sky. Her roar in my ears makes the world spin.

While my place on the planet may seem, to some, desolate and empty and dry, up close and personal it has a deep succulence and is crowded with cows and horses and wildlife. Crowded also with my husband, life partner, boss, best friend Gail Steiger, occasional grandchildren Clint and Kamber, dogs Jim and Bella, and an elk skull named Bullwinkle, propped in the corner of our living room, lit with twinkle lights year-round. Peopled, also, with the phantoms of ancient tribes that have come and gone from this place and left artifacts in layers. I write from a rocking chair in an office that is more creative cave than sterile workplace, from a cow camp cabin down in the low desert, from the smoky side of the fire, from a camp chair or tent when we sleep out on the ground as we move these cows around on public land. On many days, I write with a good horse between my knees because I earn my paycheck as a cowboy. And some days I write in a journal pulled from a backpack as I rest in a deep canyon because I love to hike in this country, solo except for the dogs and the wild things that crowd this land.

And so, in these pages, I hope you hear a clear song from this place. A song of bones and fire and water. I seek a simple melody with a drumbeat that mimics the heart, for a tune that reaches out and says, *I see you, I hear you.* Sing with me.

FINDING BULLWINKLE

Bullwinkle died alone, down by Alligator Spring. By the time I saw them, his bones were scattered in a wide circle by those whose job is to scatter bones.

When I first came to live with Gail Steiger, our exploration of each other included our very different backgrounds. We told each other our stories.

"They really believe all of that?" he has asked me many times, questions about the culture and faith from which I come, about my family of origin. The questions heightened in intensity after he met and spent time with these raucous, funny, intelligent, talkative people.

"Those smart people really believe that they are the center of the universe, that they will live forever? They really believe all that god stuff?"

No matter that my defenses rise, my bow strung and raised and pulled in honor of these people I love. No matter the hours I could spend explaining doctrine and gospel and apologetics, quoting chapter and verse. There is no defense. Just the simple answer. Yes. Yes, they not only believe but are rooted firmly in a culture based on that belief. They can't imagine not believing.

Everyone wants to be on the winning team.

Everyone dies alone. I sit on a bay mare at Alligator Spring and look at the elk carcass scattered white across the hillock where Bullwinkle died. His skull lies gracefully in the center of the circle, too heavy to be moved by the carrion-eaters. The salt on my face, dried in the wind, is not in response to having found a dead elk but rather to the text message I received an hour earlier.

For five days we have been camped in a place where there is no cell phone signal unless we top out high on a ridge. We have been gathering remnant, the left-behind cows. Every morning we saddle up to ride rough country on faint trails. My previous sense of well-being and peace might have come from the work, but the work does not always go smoothly and parts of it are arduous and discouraging. The sense of well-being may have come from sleeping and cooking and eating out-of-doors, but it is hard to roll out of bed on cold early mornings, and I like hot baths.

The poetry comes from the sound of the fire and one leg uncomfortably hot as I sit sideways to the flames, the waking-up birds waiting for the sun to begin their full-on song, pepper jack cheese melted on the morning eggs and the coffee pot propped on a handy rock. It is felt in the bite of the day when I move away from the fire. It is filthy jeans and sooty hands that will become a memory after we load up for home. It is the sound of an impatient horse pawing the feed bunk before dawn. Small critters slipping through the underbrush, rustling duff and leaves. That moment when the bulls I've been reasoning with all afternoon finally go through the gate, when I pass my tin plate through the fire twice to warm it before loading it with food. When the black horned bull paws the ground once and then puts Gail over the fence and the boss calls the massive animal *unappreciative*. When my breath condenses on the edge of the bedroll tarp and I wake with an icy patch by my chin in the night, roll over and find a new warm spot. Eggshells in the fire pit. Riding over an ancient midden and realizing that humans have always made garbage.

More than any other factor, I believe that being unplugged from the news and from social media is the reason for my increased sense of contentment during these long stretches of gathering cows surrounded by signal-blocking hills. It gets dark early this time of year, and no screens light up our nights. We read books by headlamp. We talk about what we've read and mark short stories for each other. We stand and watch the day's catch eat hay. We discuss which heifers to ship and whether that old cow is bred and if she deserves one more chance to stay around. My phone is an instrument to capture beauty—only that—and it rests on airplane mode and medium battery saver, unable to deliver *WSJ* updates or chosen-just-for-me Google cards. Bruce Springsteen and his Broadway run. Google knows what I like. But even Google can't deliver this happiness.

My ability to rest and my penchant for choosing joy are strengthened by this remove from world events pinging onto a screen. I never tell my partner to listen to a newscast the way I alerted him last night when an owl was broadcasting his story from the creek bottom, or when we heard a bull volunteering to hay after the evening fire was built. I have never stood in awe of a Facebook post the way we did when the red-tailed hawk wheeled overhead yesterday as we sat high up on a ridge. He was checking us out and had no need of our response emoji—thumbs-up or wow or love. And I have never gotten an email as exciting as that beautifully distinct bear track left for me to discover beside the creek. My heart says it is a work of art . . . but for the bear, just a step in the journey.

It is true that during these unplugged days I have no information about what is going on in the bigger world—who did what to whom, who went to war, who tweeted, who died, who lived, where the fires broke out or the waters jumped their banks. But I do know that the red droop-horned cow bawled her baby up in the night and we will have to gather the holding trap because that black steer we picked up yesterday didn't come to hay. He's up high in the boulders with the early morning sun on his back. And I know I made fried potatoes to go with our burgers—the last raw meat in a week-old cooler. And coffee boiled on the fire is stronger and richer and hotter than when we make it with electricity.

And life is precious.

But yesterday was election day. Gail and I voted by mail-in ballot weeks ago because like many people in agriculture, we are not always close to pavement and voting booths on the right day, but still wish our voices to count. Today Gail is hauling cattle to the sale barn, a six- or eight-hour round trip. He will bring us a treat tonight, sub sandwiches from the gas station deli, perhaps even a fresh bag of ice for the cooler. I am managing stock in camp and riding to Alligator Spring. Yesterday we came here and found two mama cows without their calves in tow. Today I hope to catch them on water again, this time with their babies. But we didn't know, over coffee this morning, who won the presidential election. Gail promised to send a text and if I got up high enough, I would know, too.

"I am sorry, baby." That is all it said.

For the next several months, we ask the same questions, doubting people we have known and loved for years. They really voted for him? They really thought he had the moral and intellectual capacity to lead this country?

Yes. They really did vote that way. As for moral and intellectual . . . these are not characteristics considered so much as showmanship and sensationalism.

Everyone wants to be on the winning team.

Bullwinkle died alone. Several weeks after my discovery, we rode ATVs that we call quads back to the trail above Alligator Spring, hiked down the steep slope to where his bones lay. Gail lifted the skull by one enormous antler.

He looked up at me. "He was a big ol' boy!"

He is a big ol' boy. We took turns carrying the skull uphill and tied it firmly to the yellow quad. He lives in our home, graced year-round by tiny white twinkle lights. He is my hope and my altar.

Bullwinkle is not perfect. He has only one seven-point antler, the left side of his skull deformed by an injury when he was young. The mule deer expert I spoke with assumes that it is the same as when a buck's skull is fractured in battle, and rapidly developing cells that create the rack leak into the wound. Bullwinkle grew an odd deformity on the injured side, never again a full antler. Every year he carried one heavy side and one stunted side. Even though he lived to be old, his whole frame was probably deformed from his every half a year of lopsidedness.

We are all lopsided. We all have something. We all carry a grief, an injury, that we cannot set down. The key is to recognize, name, heal that wound and carry it out into the world as a gift. Bullwinkle reminds me that this too shall pass. That I do not carry the old rugged cross from my childhood, and neither do I carry the shadow of a man who is not worthy of being my leader.

Bullwinkle reminds me of the creatures who never know of leaders or Jesuses.

Bullwinkle reminds me that we are all alone in death and there is rest in a wide circle of bones.

LOADING CHUTES AND IRRIGATION DITCHES

The fruits of his labor fall and rot slowly on the ground.
—Mary Gauthier, "Mercy Now"

"Oh, there were loading chutes on the ranch before Jim built these. They were rickety old wooden pieces of shit. Remember Whistle, that little horse I told you about? He fell through the rotten boards one time when we were loading horses in the bobtail truck. That was back when we hauled livestock all over the ranch, rather than making them walk, back when the roads were, well, *roads*."

We have unfolded chairs at one of our camps, in the late afternoon, watching storm clouds build and boil, wondering if it will rain in the night. We are sitting under a tin roof water catchment that Gail and our friend Ivan built a few years ago. It has been a game-changer in managing stock here at this confluence of three major pastures on the ranch. Every time a drop of water falls from the sky and hits this tin roof, it runs through the gutters and down a spout into a water storage. The whole set-up is called a trick tank.

When we gather cows into this little set of corrals, I admit that we are often stingy, watering horses only out of the small trough, or, sometimes, cattle we've sorted out of the herd to be hauled to the sale barn. The rest of them, when we are finished sorting and branding, must walk down the trail and into the next pasture before they get a drink. This caught water is precious. Gail has plans to build a new catchment on a very remote part of this grazing allotment, another game-changer. He looks wryly at Jim's loading chute. "I may be the only one who will appreciate the new trick tank, but I still want to get it built next spring."

Our tent is set up and the camp stove is on the table in case I need to cook using gas bottled in a canister instead of a wood fire. This is a light camp with cans of chili in the camp box and packets of precooked rice to add for interest and bulk. Oatmeal and Spam for morning. We have books and beers. I warm up our meal while he waters the horses. The thunder is so faint that we wonder for a moment if it is a hunter in a side-by-side ATV coming down the trail. We'd rather have the thunder. The cattle in the corral have almost finished chewing hay and are beginning to lie down, one by one, with sighs. It was a long day for all of us. Tomorrow Gail will back the long gooseneck trailer up to the narrow alley and haul the first load of cattle to the sale barn while I stay behind to manage the other two loads and our horses, leading them to the trough to drink every few hours.

A few weeks ago, I dug through my keepsake boxes until I found a blue plastic wristwatch with the image of Ronald Reagan on the face, a memento from the 1984 presidential election, given to me by my grandfather, just as he passed them out all over Pecos County, Texas. eBay values it at twenty dollars in an age when very few people wear watches on their wrists unless they are also Bluetoothed to their smartphones. I mail off the left-behind piece of my maternal grandfather to a dear friend who collects election memorabilia, a future decoration and conversation piece for her future office in a think tank or university. But I wanted her to know about the man who gave it to me: thirty-year county commissioner, avid campaigner for the Republican Party, active member on water boards and state government committees. And in this age of easy-to-find information I am left cold.

We have a false belief that anything can be found on the internet; that students need not learn the facts, only how to find them; that we should be teaching critical thinking and discernment as we are faced with making decisions concerning so many new global situations. But as I search for information about a man who was a community leader and achieved so much in his lifetime, who was witness to history and stories completely lost now, the only thing I can find is his obituary and that of my grandmother. Eventually I dig up one interview from later in his life in which he sounds bitter and disillusioned. The writer refers to him as "old Bill Moody" in a paragraph about the siphoning of water out of the deep artesian springs of West Texas. In the interview, my grandfather spoke of learning to dance as a teenager on the platform above free-flowing Comanche Spring. He talked of floating home, in the night, after the dancing was done, down the irrigation ditch to the family farm several miles from town, carried along with the miracle of water that made an oasis out of the desert, allowing five dairies in the area and the growing of so much produce and hay. Later, as county commissioner, he was instrumental in the beautification of those ditches, back when no one believed that Comanche Spring would ever run dry. Now the trees he planted are dead, and the beautiful rock waterways are monuments to our lack of imagination, monuments to the universal hubris of a species that robs the planet of Her abundance. The fruits of his labor lie rotting slowly on the ground.

Curious, I use the same search engine to seek the names of my other grandparents, finding only faint traces that they even lived, much less loved and laughed and gave birth and grew crops. Almost nothing of the women.

We don't use the loading chute that Jim built. It is a structure easily overlooked by someone not aware of things like bobtail trucks and the construction of chutes, of the distance to the nearest pavement or house. Or what welding steel entails. It is a work of art to someone who understands what it would take to haul the materials and equipment, to spend days in this remote location building this serviceable monument. Jim's legacy is beautifully built with much labor and expense, admirable in scope and craftsmanship and execution. And this is not the only one. These loading chutes are scattered all over this grazing allotment, at every little set of corrals.

"Did anyone ever use them?" I like it when Gail tells me stories of this place, stories that came before me.

"Oh, once or twice. I loaded cattle out of this one on the day the bobtail truck burned up."

Jim, like all of us, assumed that the world would stay the same. He assumed that the Forest Service would continue blading the roads all the way back in here, that the ranch would always have the bobtail. The loading chutes are too high off the ground to load cattle into the gooseneck stock trailer. They've been idle, these works of art, for twenty-five years.

The antique pottery bread bowl serves now only as a place to stash store-bought bread, sourdough English muffins, tortillas wrapped in plastic. I rarely fill it with pale fragrant dough as I did when I was feeding teenagers or large crews of cowboys. My former mother-in-law bought it for me during a previous season in my life. That season is gone, and so is she. Her name was Carolyn, and I write it down so my children don't forget.

This house is made of concrete—ceiling, walls, floors, and even my kitchen countertops—so when I lift the bowl to clean or, perhaps, on a holiday when I have guests coming and want to pull tray after tray of steaming crusty rolls from the oven, I am oh, so careful. I see the fine crack and hear the odd ring the bowl makes now. It is so very fragile.

I wrote about this bowl almost two decades ago at a creative process retreat in South Dakota, by coincidence not far from where my first husband was born and not far from where Carolyn lived. My editor, Andy Wilkinson, was leading the retreat, and I had ridden along with him from the Texas Panhandle for the adventure and the immersion. One morning, during a quiet time for writing, I sat in the sunny gathering room and wrote about the bread bowl. Andy rose from his own work to pull Stephen Mitchell's translation of the *Tao Te Ching* from a shelf and toss it in my lap. "You can't write that essay until you read that book." We were at a testing place in our relationship, me student, him mentor. I picked up the book with forefinger and thumb, dropped it to the floor, and went on writing.

Two weeks later, retreat over, road trip a memory as I navigated the familiar waters of home and children, a package arrived in the mail. A copy of the *Tao Te Ching*, Stephen Mitchell's version. Andy was right. The bread bowl was only a metaphor. The Tao is the eternal Tao. And I wrote.

I rarely fill the emptiness of that bowl with the ingredients of Carolyn's bread recipe now, kneading it into nutrient-filled elasticity, the process as precious as the product. And I wonder if I should put a label on the bottom of the bowl: *This is the bowl I wrote about in* Rightful Place. I feel like an old lady wandering around her house full of treasures wondering if anyone will treasure them after she is gone . . . or simply sort them into boxes to haul to the dump or Goodwill, keeping only a few small mementoes. The bowl will one day be in pieces, pottery sherds like those scattered over this land, traces of a culture that disappeared from this region around the time the Anasazi disappeared from the Four Corners region. Fragments of earth going back to the earth.

Will anyone new ever find that first book I wrote, *Rightful Place*, on some dusty shelf? Will it stay in print in this digital age? A book of essays, one of millions. A book, one of trillions, so many forgotten with time.

This summer I held a friend's hand as her first book was released by a small independent press, the release date like a baby's due date, a nebulous guess. The week that it finally shipped out to readers, she agonized. I looked at my own shelf with five books bearing my own name and warned her gently, "The book is not you. It is a project that you worked on. Only that. Remove your ego from the book release."

Do your job and step back. Thank you, Lao Tzu.

What is our legacy? What do we leave behind us? The songs Gail has written may disappear just as my Hale grandfather's stories are faint echoes in our family past. I'll leave their grandmother's bread recipe to my daughter and son. I'll tell them the story of Bill Moody demanding that his sixteen-year-old daughter, my mother, get a summer job and when she ignored him, he found her a gig hoeing cotton in the June sun of West Texas. It only took her a week to find a position as lifeguard at the Comanche Spring swimming pool. His legacy, his influence, makes us stronger as a family and as individuals, lessons of the past passed along.

We stand in the middle of life and think of what we as individuals will leave behind us, and some of us ponder what we as a species are leaving behind as our legacy on the earth. In *The World Without Us*, Alan Weisman posits that this glorious planet will reclaim Herself and break down most of the human-built structures when people are gone. But in our pondering, we may consider that kind words and a handwritten note in the mail are a sort of legacy as well. Maybe not as solid as a steel loading chute with unspoiled wooden decking, used once or twice before being abandoned because of a dozen esoteric details, meaningless to those ungrounded in a specific place or profession or understanding. It bakes day after day in the Arizona sun, unharvested scrap metal, or, if Weisman is right, a structure to be dissolved and absorbed over so many years that our brains find it hard to comprehend. Will a writer's lifework also blow away in the wind? Words words words, our precious words, now meaningless or forgotten. And does it matter? Does the fleeting nature of our legacy keep us from dragging a welder on rubber tires into the backcountry and sleeping there until the job is done? It won't keep Gail from building another water catchment in the desert or writing a new song. It didn't keep my grandfather from doing his part to beautify his community or fight for what he thought was right, even if that legacy cannot be found on the World Wide Web. Does it keep us from making homemade cinnamon rolls for Christmas morning in a cracked pottery bread bowl? Does it keep me from picking up my pen and writing about work and life?

Our work is not eternal, but it is worth doing, and so we rise. We pick up our tools and we do what we can, in this moment. And we make a difference.

HOLISTIC AND HELL

Everything changes, that's what they say. Yesterday's gone or fading away.

—Gail Steiger, "I See a Rider"

"Careful what you ask for." He's repeated the phrase many times today.

We are watching the mountain burn.

My post on Instagram might possibly show my talent for capturing drama with a smartphone, but as my photographer friend Jessica points out, it is hard to take a bad picture in the light thrown from a forest fire. The picture shows Gail as ranch manager, facing the flames, his back to me, smoke turning the sky orange, blanking out the sun. He's worn the same shirt for three days and his work hat is filthy.

Yesterday we gathered cows with ash falling from the sky. Today we stand on the rim of a mesa and watch a monster eat its way over the ridges, devouring everything in its path, beloved landmarks in our backyard though we are miles from ranch headquarters, our actual home. Now I understand why they say fire is alive.

It is as dramatic as it sounds and looks, and the explanations are exhausting. We chose this, as much as we were offered a choice. Ten days ago, lightning struck Cedar Mesa, making a twelve-acre footprint. USFS policy states that a fire can be used for range improvement if it is initiated by nature. *Managed* is the word they use. So yesterday, after ten days of wind and rapidly dropping humidity, the Forest Service reignited the footprint. Now our world is burning.

Careful what you ask for.

With permission granted by the range conservationist (our direct overseer within the US Forest Service), Gail and John, a friend and dayworker, and I moved into camp to gather cows from the top of another mesa. We looked at the bright clear sky and laughed. *Wonder where their fire is?* A few hours later we had stopped laughing. Purgatory conditions, hot and so very dry, with a persistent wind, had made their fire. Helicopters trailed back and forth above us, and I mistakenly thought they were carrying water. What I thought were buckets looked so small, as if they were throwing tablespoons on a burning house. Later I found out that what I saw dangling beneath the helicopters were not buckets but propane torches, flamethrowers, and it seems contrary to everything that is right.

When we got to the holding trap with the cows, John and I watered the horses and started setting up camp while Gail hiked to a high point where cell phones reach a signal so he could call our range con who had told us to go ahead and move into camp when they spoke from headquarters early that morning. The story had changed with the day. He came back to camp and said, "We have to leave. This fire is bigger and hotter than they expected." It took two hours for John and me to ride back to headquarters, leading Gail's horse. Gail hiked down to the second camp we had located to drive the pickup and gooseneck trailer out of the backcountry. He got in after midnight. We left the cows behind.

Careful what you ask for.

Yellow-shirted government employees in so many different vehicles kept arriving at ranch headquarters and the phone calls were nonstop. My dog, Jim, got tired of strangers and sat on my feet with a low grumble in his throat. The fire was so far from here, or any structure, as to be laughable, but they wanted Gail's opinion. What should burn and where should they drop fire? For twenty years Gail has spoken about the last time parts of this ranch burned and the beauty of regrowth, of water bubbling up in springs that hadn't existed before, of palatable new growth of browse where most of the cows and wildlife could be found as the land recovered, nutrients and seeds driven deep into the soil, bringing up the lush green. Every year he has advocated, to no avail, for burning to make more of the land usable for grazing so we can rest the pieces that get too much use. Every year he sits in meetings hoping for exactly what we stood witnessing from the rim.

Careful what you ask for.

The word holistic comes into play, always the biggest, most complicated word in our world. In medicine, doctors use the word holistic in relation to looking at the whole person—body, soul, spirit, mind, emotion, will, environment, culture, past traumas, current hopes, future dreams. I wish it were that simple here.

Simply put, holistic means compromise.

The decisions begin a long time before we saddle up to ride. Are the horses shod? Who will ride which horse and what are the jobs at hand? And BB is better to rope on than Linda, and Roscoe is showing his age and needs the shorter days, but on this ranch, there is no guarantee of how long the job will take. I make lists upon lists, always considering how many people will be in each camp and for how many nights and for how many breakfasts and make sure we have enough chairs and an extra in case one breaks or blows over into the fire. Spare headlamp batteries in the camp box. Benadryl and ibuprofen and toilet paper. Layer the food into the coolers so that the first night's meal is on top. How many bales of hay in each trailer? Branding rig with blood-stop powder and needles and vaccines and will it stay cool enough until we get there with our gather in four days? Fill the propane bottles while we are in town and buy Bickmore salve in case someone sores a horse's back.

Where should we move the cows? That decision often ends up being the most difficult because of questions of water and utilization. Do we make the best decision for the cows or for the land, and who decides? When we ride out, we try to see and think about each plant, hundreds of species struggling to rise in spite of inadequate carbohydrate stores or rainfall. Organic matter and microbes in the soil. Each cow and her offspring, past, present, and future. Each critter in this country coming closer and closer to our camps to drink during drought. The Forest Service and their oversight. Other agencies like Arizona Game and Fish and NRCS. The owner of the ranch who signs our paychecks and his history with Gail, hundreds of cups of coffee on hundreds of Saturday afternoons, and his eye on the bottom line. The markets, enormous and complicated and mercurial, beyond our control. The forecast and the currents of air in the oceans, so far from our piece of desert. The men I ride with. The one I sleep with; stress is an unwelcome bedfellow. The logistics of branding longears and hauling shippers to the sale barn, a nine-hour round trip with gooseneck trailers from the corrals where we stashed that second camp.

My monthly cycle and planning ahead for the possibility of menses while we are riding long hours and sleeping out.

The weather. Always the weather.

And now, this fire. It is a scientific and logistical hell. A managed, prescribed, and controlled hell, at least on paper and with constant talk, talk, talk. Everyone has a plan and a protocol. They all have maps, speaking in terms I don't understand using trail and quadrant designations, section numbers marked on a broad flat piece of paper to illustrate and designate country that is anything but flat.

> Section 17. Trail 11. Gail turns to me, translating, "You know . . . over there where we saw that bee tree that the bear tore open." Ah, yes. There. The bee tree and the honey and the bear all gone.

Section 47. "Where you found Bullwinkle." Yes, fire will help the country over there. Run, you old elk who've lived there all your lives. Please don't let the fire burn all the way to the beaver dam.

Section 21. "Where we drove those cows off that ridge that day," and we didn't even know there was a trail and we had to lead our horses because it was so steep. Yes, I remember . . . rocks and dirt sliding beneath feet and hooves, a long way down.

Section 14. "That's where we put cows a week ago. Don't drop fire in that quadrant. Draw a big square around it. No, bigger, draw a bigger square around it." I think of the zone-tailed hawk nesting down by the spring. She and Gail sang back and forth to each other while he rebuilt the water gap. The fence between us and the neighboring ranch is gone now.

Section 32. Where we saw that lion track by the wire gate.

Section 16. Bobcat Spring where I found the atlatl point.

The list goes on and they are on fire, these men and women earning time and a half here at the end of fire season.

Careful what you ask for.

We will witness recovery. Fences can be rebuilt, even in country this rough.

Will we find dead cows and wildlife when we ride in the black of the burn? Maybe. Will there be rejoicing in our heaven when the water rises and the seep springs spring back up because of fewer leaves drinking? Sure. Will I take photos of the green and post them on Instagram? I hope so.

Our range con called. They've pulled the crews and dismantled the hierarchy surrounding this fire, and I am sure InciWeb says everything is fully contained. The big equipment and helicopters and tanker trucks have gone home. They are in the mop-up stages, which is what I have been doing at home since being grounded from working cows, cleaning everything in sight. The range con says we are allowed limited access back onto the public land.

My grandson went with Gail to spot a camp so we can start moving cows again. He is horrified. His four-year-old mind cannot imagine why his grampa allowed the country to burn. They stopped and tasted the sweet new growth at the bottom of the oakbrush. Then they tasted the harsh old growth on a plant outside the burn. This is a lesson I would never have considered giving him, empathy with the ungulates that eat the browse. That empathy is more important than all the science. They spit out the chewed-up leaves and the story told in four-year-old language is sweet.

Today is Sunday. I am home alone, worshiping with coffee and ice water and vine-ripe tomatoes, the first spaghetti squash and a very clean house. A chipmunk runs down the wall and jumps over into the oak tree where the seed tray hosts a congregation. As soon as her face is puffed with seeds, she climbs back onto the roof where I am sure she has a nest inside the chimney of the wood stove. I wish I could explain fire and smoke to her, but experience is the best teacher.

The cat-faced orb weavers under the eaves are round and fat with eggs, part of their cycle here at the end of their days. The hummingbirds are emptying the feeders of sweet. The forecast is for 79 degrees today, a delivery from 90-plus. From where I sit, I can feel the cooler air on my bare arms because it is still open-window weather.

We are asking for rain.

DRINKING
WILD WATER

When I pack my duffel for camp, I slip in a white enamelware mug painted with flowers, decidedly feminine compared to the blue tin cups in the camp box. I clip it on my pack when I load up for a hike, and when I am shouldering through the hard parts, I hear its comforting clink. The friend who gave it to me wanted me to have one with a white interior so I could see the bits of plant and animal life when I scoop water from the creeks. What she doesn't know is that I don't care; I drink them straight down. The branches of these creeks have become part of me.

While we encourage others to use a filter, Gail and I drink from these streams often. We know the source of this water; we know what is upstream. Our bodies have developed the flora and fauna to handle the bugs that are here.

Distillers of bourbon in Kentucky and Tennessee would often bottle the creek water used in the distillation process so that when a bartender offered a customer a splash to dilute the drink, the water was as close as possible to the original source of the bourbon itself.

So many details make up our lives and our experience. What we carry with us is dictated by where we are going and for how long. Intimacy with our landscape, both inner and outer, dictates how we move in the world. Who we are on the inside informs where we feel safe to drink and sleep and live.

So many things are handed to us daily. The exhausted among us are those who are either perpetually sleeping or those who are constantly doing, serving, carrying, solving things that do not belong to them. The noise is frightful. Click here. Like this. Recycle. Follow me. Drive a hybrid. Eat kale. Juice. Buy Me. Don't let the laundry sour in the washer. Mommy, tie my shoe. Read this. Answer every email. Listen to me. Heal me. Save me. Love me. Pat me. Where are my glasses? What time is the game? When do we eat? What do we do with thirty-eight sacks of concrete?

A problem handed to me. Perhaps it is not mine to solve. Perhaps it is not even a problem. Perhaps it is just thirty-eight sacks of concrete. Nothing more.

It is not necessary to act on all information received. There is a finite amount of energy in the universe and as it swirls 'round and 'round, we are able to channel only a certain cupful through our creative spans. If we are lucky, we spend the first half of our lives waking up and figuring out where our energy is best spent—for the good of the species and the planet and our nearer community. Or maybe in service to the work itself because we have fallen in love.

I want to be one whose eyes are open, scanning the ground as well as the horizon, whose ears are pointed straight up listening for new songs, whose nose reads the changes in the wind while the pads of my feet read the stories beneath the crust. There are days when duty and obligation make us feel pulled, like taffy, in all directions, becoming stiffer and stiffer until we are brittle thin and some of our starfish arms break away. I drink creek water as antidote.

What would I show you if I could?

Twenty yards of barbed wire fence lying on the ground between us and the ranch to the north . . . and we're thirty head short of our cow count. I have a manuscript to edit, and we have more rough country to ride, more cows to gather and move.

I would show you how I am scared that I don't work hard enough. I would show you two folding chairs at cow camp, fire at our feet and in the evening sky, cows moving slowly up into the holding trap as deer come to the dam to drink while out on the rim three coyotes sing, sounding like a chorus of thirty. I would show you, on some nights, my body so tired that it aches and a sky so big and unpolluted that I must close my eyes. I would show you my need to celebrate the day just past. So I pour bourbon in that tin cup as the sun goes down, a marker to say it is okay to stop working, a marker to say stand down, have a small party, celebrate.

I add a splash of branch, that wild intoxicating water that sustains me along my way.

Bartender, please, wild water on the rocks.

POVERTY MENTALITY

Last night I found out that my grandchildren, Clint and Kamber, who have been here at the ranch with us for three days, will be with us for three more. I panicked. We are out of kid food and it is forty-five miles to town, and it feels horribly irresponsible, not to mention exhausting, to take two small children to the grocery store during a pandemic just because Mamie is out of fruit and string cheese.

My panic throws me back to the mid-nineties when I was raising my own children on a remote ranch in the Texas river-break country. The house we lived in was horrible. I struggled to keep the children warm with a wood-burning stove and open-flame propane heaters, the illegal kind with decorative asbestos bricks. I tore old blankets into strips to fill gaps in the leaky window frames, in winter to keep out the cold and year-round to keep out the blowing barnyard dirt. I threw boxes of mothballs under the old house set up on cement blocks to keep the skunks and rattlesnakes from making nests beneath our feet. The well water contained gypsum, a mineral that made it nonpotable, so we drank from an ancient rainwater cistern with a charcoal filter, the water hauled up from the black depths in a metal bucket, hand over hand. I struggled, in those years, to feed our family on below-poverty wages. I struggled to homeschool those children, so many miles from town, budgeting carefully for learning materials. I struggled to keep them safe from rattlesnakes and feral hogs, to seek out appropriate social opportunities, to grow a few

33

straggling flowers, mainly moss roses and marigolds and violas, to be kind and patient when the struggling wore me out.

Everything seems harder with no money.

During that time in my life, living on that ranch, in that horrible little house, my best friend Shellie was a bright shining light. We met when we were both eighteen and living in Knapp Hall on the campus of Texas Tech University. I only stayed two semesters before getting married, but she continued on with university, coming out to the ranch some weekends. I prepared so carefully for her visits, planning the menus to be almost labor free so I could enjoy another woman in my life, but also making sure we had a touch of elegance like fresh vegetables and dips, which may have seemed commonplace to her but were a luxury for me. She brought with her VHS recordings of the popular television sitcom *Friends*, carefully labeled with season and episodes. We didn't have a telephone way out there on the remote ranch camp, much less a satellite dish for television reception. On her next visit, she would bring the next batch of tapes, sometimes with attached episodes of *Mad About You* if she forgot to stop recording when the credits rolled on Central Perk.

Like social media today, that sitcom gave me a false image of what life away from my own was like. I even imagined that Shellie's life was like those of our fictional friends in New York City. I imagined that what I saw on the screen was everything I was missing out on by having chosen marriage and babies and an unconventional rural life miles from the pavement rather than an education, a career, something more normal. My life felt like drudgery in contrast to what I saw on the screen, and it smelled of cloth diapers, cow shit, and the ever-present pot of pinto beans simmering on the stove. I watched Monica, Rachel, Phoebe, Ross, Chandler, and Joey chatting over coffee, going on dates, making jokes with cute clothes, romance, and problems that didn't seem like real problems. And everything was so clean! Even when Rachel cut up her credit cards, going out into the world on her own without Daddy's money, her heart didn't break in the night wondering how she would feed small children with quarters fished from the change jar at the end of the month, the pediatrician's warning that they needed more fresh fruits and vegetables ringing in her ears. And though Monica was a chef, the show never showed the sheer labor of buying groceries in the city eighty miles away, hauling them home, then cooking for crews of fifteen cowboys in a kitchen the size of a pocket handkerchief, hauling the food over rough dirt roads to the corrals, infant strapped into a car seat, toddler with a dirty face. She never washed mountains of dishes on a June afternoon, the only cool a waft of fetid air from a swamp cooler, only to get up at three a.m. the next day to do it all over again. And the men on the show were not always weary and dirty or checking heavy-bred heifers in the cold at two in the morning. Never once did the women on the show fetch the guys a beer.

Today, social media, like that television show, often highlights our poverty, our lack, our deficits. It shows us how special everyone else is and all that we do not have. Currently, social media highlights the deficits within our society. Big gaping holes become evident. Some people slept through seventh-grade grammar. *Lie means to recline; lay means to place.* During this pandemic, ignorance of basic biology and other sciences are highlighted with memes. And some people are blind to the history of this nation. We are the out-of-context generation.

A poverty mentality is a paucity of imagination.

True poverty, that which threatens survival, leaves a stain behind even after the pressure lifts and a new season commences. Poverty strikes a blow to innocence, to trust, to hope, to ambition when every single day and decision seem uphill. Poverty makes it hard to relax our shoulders from up around our ears. The stain left behind is a greasy reminder of those long dark days when worry and hunger, physical in some instances, and spiritual in most, predominated every thought. It is hard to suck the marrow from the bones during the good times when the memory of lean years makes us want to tuck pieces of meat and marrow away in case the winter comes again.

I didn't grow up in poverty, and I have no idea why I grew up thinking we were poor. My parents both have college educations and came from middle-class white America. The stories of living through the Depression and putting milk cans on trains, those same cans returning empty with payment in the bottom, the stories of butchering for the local grocery store in the evenings in exchange for dented canned goods, the stories of buying livestock on specu-lation and grazing the barrow ditches . . . those stories were from my grandparents' generation. They made a better life for their chil-dren. My mother stayed home to birth and raise the four of us, but she went back to teaching when I was in high school. We were a two-income family after that. My father bounced from passion to passion: teaching, ranching, shoeing horses, working in the oil field as a contractor and then as a well analyst, even once selling World Book encyclopedias door to door when oil prices plummeted. But they always owned our home, even when he went back to college to preach the Christian gospel on a college campus, studying for a master's degree he never finished. We always had food, and, I realize now, the plain and unimaginative nature of our meals had more to do with my mother's personality than with finances. It had to do more with West Texas culture than money. We always had a nice clean warm home and suitable clothing. So why did I grow up thinking we were poor?

My father was the only one who spent money with impunity because he was the one who earned it. Even when my mother went back to work as a seventh-grade English teacher, she was parsimonious. She justified every single item she put in the grocery cart and then repeated her reasons again as we unloaded the brown paper sacks at home, even if my father was nowhere within earshot. Money and finances were a big deal in our home. Wanting something, like shoes, from the JCPenney catalog, was a big deal. Asking for a new dress for prom in high school was a big deal and met with disapproval. And yet, no one educated us about money or investing or saving or filing taxes. Borrowing and debt were akin to saying a bad word. We didn't fucking do that in our family.

I remember words easily, but numbers rarely.

It was a Saturday morning, and, under my mother's direction, we were cleaning my grandparents' house. I was dusting the furniture in the silence that lay like a blanket smothering last night's heated argument between my father and my grandfather. They had stood toe to toe, shouting at each other. My father learned this skill from his father, both the volume and how to argue. Like father, like son. The loudest person wins.

I moved the Pledge-scented cloth over the smooth wood of the hutch until it touched the edge of the check. My father had written that check to my grandfather during their fight as if money could heal the wounds made by their words, wielded efficiently, like swords. He was living with his parents temporarily until he and my mother could sell our house in Van Horn and move to Fort Stockton, to the oil boom. My mother drove us over on Fridays after school, 120 miles. We would watch the horizon for the red barn on the top of the hill on the outskirts of town and sing out "I see the red barn!" as a signal that the two-hour drive was almost over.

My grandfather was angry at my parents for hiring a babysitter the night before so they could go out on a date. He thought we'd be staying there with him and Granny. My parents thought four children were too much for them to handle. But it didn't matter to me what the fight was about. I was eleven years old. What I cared about was that check, written in anger. It was four digits, though of course I don't remember which four. I knew nothing about money, and it seemed a huge amount, a break-the-bank, we-can-never-buy-food-again amount.

I slipped the check into my pocket when no one was looking. I finished the dusting while my mother ran the vacuum, sucking bad will from the air. When the chores were done, I asked if I could go for a walk. I crossed the street into a vacant lot where I surreptitiously tore one tiny bit of that check off at a time and let it blow away in the West Texas wind until there was no more rectangular piece of paper with my father's slanted handwriting and the power of destitution.

Later in the day, the adults searched for the check. They even moved the hutch out away from the wall, asking me if I had seen it, and I shook my head no, sneaky to the end. My father, jovial and kind as he always is after losing his temper, said no problem. He'd just cancel that one with the bank and write another. I don't know if he ever did.

I read somewhere that money is an exchange of energy. What energy blew away in that wind?

I got married at nineteen years old, already carrying a poverty mentality, that concept of never enough, but it wasn't until I began living on cowboy wages with my new husband that I experienced actual poverty, the stretching of every penny so we could eat and put gas in the truck. The struggle to feed my babies. The application process for Medicaid, WIC, and food stamps in offices where the social workers were ever so slightly disdainful. The hand-me-downs and worry over nutrition. The lack of health insurance. The stress that was Christmas, every . . . single . . . goddamned . . . year. The homelessness when my husband got fired or got mad and quit his job, because our housing came with his cowboy employment and when we moved on to the next ranch, I never knew what kind of lodging I faced, what kind of filth, what kind of struggle to get the owner or ranch manager to turn loose of the purse strings for simple things like paint or new windows.

All these years later, Clint and Kamber cheer when Grampa Gail comes in the door laden with grocery bags. Blood means very little in relationships, and they adore him. He went shopping for us, buying kid food using his guiding philosophy: *If a little is good, a lot is better.* He rarely looks at the price tag on anything. He embraces abundance and often teases me, asking me when was the last time I starved to death.

As I begin putting away groceries, Kamber and Clint clamor for grapes. My poverty mentality rises again. What if we run out? My husband shares a grin with Clint and says, "Well, then, Mamie, I'll go back to Safeway!"

CULTURAL ORPHAN
BEGS A YÉI

The Navaho believe that no evil can come from the east. Some of their divinities are known as yéii, which can be translated as both *god* and *genius*. My favorite is the rainbow yéi, a water-sprinkling, dancing, protective trickster.

My friend Ivan is Navaho. He brought one of his elders to the ranch to help on a fencing project. That evening, we sat around the table, sharing a meal. Ivan told me a few days later, as we tied stays into the stretch of new fence, side by side, that it was the first time Ray had ever eaten at a white person's table.

Have we eaten in another's kitchen, someone with a deep ancestral wound? Have we spent countless evenings in conversation and laughter, an even exchange? Have we dug post holes in hard ground in summertime, side by side, together laboring? Who are we in the relationship? Have we gone to the county jail to bail out one of our own and stood side by side with a Hopi family as they sought to pawn one of their family treasures so they might take their daughter home, their young granddaughter acting as translator? Did we understand what pawn means to them? Are we breaking bread in communion or standing in a store in our pretty clothes with money in our pockets? Are we buying?

We have nothing to sell, and we do not live in poverty, a poverty caused by and perpetuated by our own race.

In a gift shop in a town surrounded by stone, the money and the sacred change hands (of course, she is nice to us, her children are hungry). We walk down the street to sit in a bar where she would not go and set a glass of red wine on the teakwood, her symbol hanging around our necks. She goes home to three grandchildren dumped on her by a crackhead daughter. She feeds them McDonald's from a sack even though the social worker has told her fresh foods are better (they cost twice as much in this redrock town) than French fries that never decay and sodas that deliver high fructose corn syrup comfort.

It was a fair exchange. Write in your journal tonight about the spirit guides she no longer hears. She doesn't have time to listen.

An impoverished orphaned spirit roams the earth, seeking graves of abolished cultures—or those that gasp and sell their sacred gods beside desert highways. They give away their shy smiles and catch-phrases because the shiny cars and well-fed pockets leave behind sugar and dollars. At night the children use sandpaper to scrub away "made in China" stamps. The teenagers paint bigger signs for the highway intersections. Authentic Indian Jewelry Ahead.

I see god in this planet, in this solar system, in this universe, in you, in me, in the earthworm, in the dense network of tree roots, in the waves, in the plankton, in the conversation at the breakfast table about buying bananas and half-and-half at the grocery store. I do not worship the animals, though I have been worshipful at sunrises and sunsets and births—and deaths. The animals have messages for me—but so do you. So does every circumstance. Perhaps I am one of Buddha's.

I won't get a Kokopelli or sugar skull tattooed on my skin, even though I love both images. Those symbols don't belong to me.

The fox tattooed on my inner wrist killed my whole flock of chickens in a month's time, left carnage behind her as she fed her young. The boar javelina would have sliced me open as easily and readily as he sliced open my dog's chest, and so my view of the benevolent Mother needed an adjustment. As someone who not only sees Pan in all things but also lives in his den, I resent those who talk about the moon but have never slept on the ground beneath her face, never done the hard journey that intimacy with the Mother requires.

How long did you sit by the waterfall? On a bench provided by the Park Service.

The laughing pocket Buddha says for me to see the privileged white woman in a place of commerce, purchasing the sacred symbols, online or in person, as a lesson in what I myself am willing to sell of my own sacred self.

How much I am willing to speak about the bear or the moon.

I am a cultural orphan, separated from the land of my generational origins, planted firmly in a land that was taken by force, by hunger, by guns, by encroachment, by theft, by enslavement, by rape and murder and pillage and squatting. By Manifest Destiny.

I have nothing to cherish from my heritage. I have no heritage other than the color of my skin.

I have given up the holy book that dictates the days and the feasts and the gifts and the attendance of my childhood. There wasn't much dancing, even when I had perfect attendance.

I have given up my flag, even as it waves overhead, and dream of living afloat on the Sea of Cortez, flagless. I have no desire to hold tightly to my weapons, and there are no symbols left when the rituals are gone.

I fast, listening to no law other than the dictates of my body.

My ancestors were squatters and slave owners. It is a beautiful thing to lay aside those symbols and doctrines which no longer serve me. I seek the Mother and She shows me her fangs. I move along, recognizing that She goes along, whether I squat on her creekbanks or not.

Standing in the kitchen, I say something about having no culture. My husband refers to where I come from by saying, "They have a culture. Show up when the bell rings and do what the teacher says."

I try to keep my voice steady. "But I am a cultural orphan."

I have *wild and precious* tattooed on my skin because poetry. Perhaps the indigent have always carved their symbols out of wood or hammered them into stone. Or inked them onto their skin.

I turn and face the east, a cultural beggar, holding out my cup, asking if I might borrow a yéi or two.

A POT OF COFFEE
AND TOBACCO FOR
HIS PIPE

Name changed to protect someone I love. I chose the name Sam in honor of Sam Seeley who showed me, one blistering hot afternoon in Bridgeport, California, what love, compassion, and charity can look like. Sam was only a young boy at the time, proving that teachers come in all ages. Thank you, Sam. This essay is dedicated to you.

Water for my horses is all I'm asking.
                              —Hoyt Axton, "Water for My Horses"

H is name is Sam.
     I first heard about him via text message from the foreman of the neighboring ranch. A hunter had encountered a backpacker off in Pine Creek who was "batshit crazy." The dogs barked midmorning on an early April day at Spider Ranch headquarters, and I walked out into the gradually warming sun.

His name is Sam.

He isn't crazy; he's malnourished, penniless, unhoused, desperate, shoved to the edges of capitalism. He faced two barking dogs, not able to see tails wagging and welcoming in the moment, and a woman with a gun in her back pocket, not able to see that I am not the type to kick him "off my land" or call the sheriff. Rather, after about five minutes of chatting, Bella licked him on the hand and Jim claimed him by sitting on his feet, assuring me that the rumors about him were wrong. I said, "First thing we need to do is get some food in you. Then we can discuss where we go from here."

Sam is not batshit crazy. He is hopeless. The last of his hope drained away with the last gallon of gas in his motorcycle, abandoned in the desert. "Out of money. Out of food. Better to die out there than in a town." He shrugs. The details slowly pile up. For sixteen days he has been hiking in very rough country, staying close to the creek, living on nopales or cactus pads, eight ounces of chocolate, a handful of mints, and some granola bars the hunter gave him. He has been hiking, not in the recreational sense, but in canyon bottoms where I have only gone for five or six days at a time, always carrying ample food, expensive freeze-dried backpacker meals, tiny tubes of coffee, nuts, fruit, and a firm sense of where I am on the map, rescue available with the press of a button.

His name is Sam.

He isn't someone in the margins, begging on the street for a dollar or a crust of bread, seeking shelter beneath bridges at night, sitting like a bundle of rags against the wall. He is a human being with a name, a story, a history, a set of skills, a sense of humor. He has unnamable wounds, and a carefully protected waterproof pouch of documents he is unable to read.

He squats beside his pack outside while I fry bacon and call Gail who is at a meeting in town. Gail says Sam should hang out in the bunkhouse until he gets home. I carry the plate of food and Sam

46

reshoulders his pack; we walk together.

"I don't do any drugs. Sometimes I smoke a little loose tobacco in a pipe but I'm all out." I say, "Let me text Gail and get him to pick some up on his way home." Sam looks at me with tears in his eyes. "You'd do that?"

When Gail shows up, he says, "First thing we need to do is find out if your bike is still there. Then we can make a plan."

The bike is right where Sam left it, sixteen days prior, as are his belongings . . . a beard trimmer, extra boots, his toothbrush, some clothing. A small glimmer of hope for someone who has nothing else to lose.

After the guys get back from their trip to retrieve the motorcycle, the three of us celebrate over the bake-at-home pizza Gail bought earlier. Sam makes us laugh by telling us he thought about eating one of his own fingers after three days with no food, gesturing at his index finger, macabre humor.

A friend asks if I was scared when Sam walked up. No. I am the one with a gun in my hip pocket and what amounts to a powerful computer in the other. I am the one who is strong and fit, well-fed— just ask the scales. I am the one with two loyal dogs at my feet, a warm home, a rich full life, and adequate (if meager) bank account, a safety net of family, friends, and employers who would lift me if I fell. I am the one with the power to help my fellow human. I am the one with wheels and fuel and a shopping list. I am the one with room to give. No, I wasn't scared.

Sam tells me that before he started his trek, going nowhere in the wilderness, he had been living on peanut butter snack crackers for several days. He hasn't had fresh food for a very long time, mainly eating out of cans, one a day; eat the whole thing, "because, you know, no refrigeration."

For days my fingers fly over the keyboard in recognition of priv-ilege, in exploration of a society that offers very few toeholds for those who have fallen and need help rising back up. I simmer with fury that poverty has been criminalized and those who are suffering are maligned. I write about my own support network, both the one I was born into through no merit of my own and the one I have cultivated consciously. And sometimes at a price. Questions of mental health and whether stress and poverty and food anxiety and lack of hope cause cognition issues, and how tangled it all is, constitute a chicken/egg puzzle that isn't mine to solve.

I write about abstract concepts like dignity and hope and safety and the human condition and worth and value, while discussing functional adult illiteracy with my daughter, Lily, who has some education and insight in this field. The abstract concepts are not as important as the concrete details of a found motorcycle, a warm bed, a pile of firewood, a welcoming smile. Kindness.

I buy Sam a four-pack of new underwear, some socks, shampoo, Irish Spring with aloe, strawberry jelly, a bag of pinto beans, a box of cookies. A travel alarm clock from True Value Hardware, a hard-to-find item when "everyone" has a phone to use as a timepiece. Which is to say I exchange some of my energy for some dignity, carried into another's space in a swirl of activity.

I am here.

That is all.

What I have "done" is so close to the bare bones. I cooked bacon (two slices), eggs (three, scrambled with cheese), toast (two slices, with apricot preserves), served on a tin plate, just a drop of my abundance, at eleven a.m. on a Wednesday.

What I have "done" is listen, offer a shower and a clean towel, a safe place, respite.

What I have "done" is carry a pillow into the bunkhouse and ask Sam if he wants to use my phone to call someone from his past.

I am piecing together his pain—his search for a job running heavy equipment but the impossibility of finding a place to sleep while he worked toward that first paycheck.

I am piecing together his despair—how much can one person

lose in a lifetime? To the point where dying of starvation in the wilderness is preferable to the indignity and danger of living in town, on charity.

I am piecing together the dehumanization in order to find the human—it has been two years since he had a place "where he could be at home."

All we have done is show him some tools, point him toward some falling-down barbed wire fence, a way to demonstrate his value and his worth, paying him for his labor with the bare bones . . . food, shelter . . . seeing him, hearing him, offering a hand in this crazy world. This messy life.

Gail and I are in the horse lot, shoeing up so we can start gathering and moving cows. It is a beautiful April morning, finally warming up. Sam walks over from where he has been cutting brush out of the horse pasture fence to ask a question about the job he is doing and the tools for his use.

Sam made a pot of coffee this morning, his first in two years. He stands in the golden sunshine and tells us what a pleasure it was to drink that coffee, put another log on the fire, and welcome this April day. "It's the small things, you know?"

Will Sam let me down as I have been let down before by my faith in humanity? That is not my business. As Mary Oliver so beautifully states, "My work is loving the world." Besides, I have already been let down by a culture and societal structure that marginalize and malign the Sams of this world. No, it isn't my business what Sam does with what he's been offered, though I am a little worried that he won't eat enough out of fear that he'll run out of food. He'll have to learn to trust us just as we will have to learn to trust him.

Meanwhile, he wakes again tomorrow with the dignity of a pot of coffee and a little tobacco for his pipe.

His name is Sam.

DIRT UNDER MY FINGERNAILS

It ain't what you're wearing. It's what you can do.
—Gail Steiger, "A Cowboy's Prayer"

I have lived and worked on commercial cattle operations since I was nineteen. While that fact seems from the outside to be quite romantic, it isn't. It has become my little joke that everyone wants a cowboy until they get one.

Now it seems, everyone wants to *be* a cowboy.

Social media is in an uproar, as social media always is, and what we hear in those spaces depends on where we are standing. This morning, the noise from my corner of the micro-population is some controversy about an R&B artist releasing a country music album, and I could not care less, other than to be unutterably grateful that I am free and able to turn off the noise and not be threatened by opinion.

Social media is a scary place. And the scariest part is the energy suck, the vampirical ability to remove us from reality, to separate us from our peace, to cause us to doubt our own selves, our own identity. The truth is, it isn't our business what other people think or believe. It isn't our business what is going on in the digital world. We are responsible for our own authenticity, our own message, our own reach, the creation of our own inner reality, our own emotions, our own skill set or lack thereof, our own peace and happiness. We must guard them closely, since our energy and our days are finite.

Our reality is defined by language, just as the canine world is defined by pack and scent. I don't look like a cowboy. I am the wrong gender for the word. I don't dress "right," when I go out in public or on the stage, and other than performing spoken word at some cowboy poetry gatherings, I don't participate in the social activities of the culture very often. I don't like rodeo because I like cows. A lot.

Cowboy is a set of skills that varies from region to region. I have some of them, am sadly lacking in others. I don't care much about social media influencers because I am too busy doing a hard job with or without "traditions," which can be chains to bind us to antiquated and arbitrary ways, to hold us down and back.

Much of what I do—if not all—is hidden . . . no pavement or arena for miles. We do not compete with others, and showing off out here is dangerous. No crew bigger than three or four. No witnesses. Just work. Just miles and miles with a horse between my knees. Just calf after calf, roped and turned loose again. Just stewardship. Just a lot of actual sweat and dirt and smoke and nights sleeping on the ground. Just doing a job. Cowboying.

And every time I re-coil my blood- and shit-covered rope, secure it back on my saddle horn, step off and loosen my cinches, every time I close that nondescript wire gate miles from any crowd behind the remnant that are finally in the right place now that we have read the ground and followed tracks until we find cows standing in those tracks, every time I finally ride back to headquarters with no words to describe the last ten days, I let go, again, of what anyone else thinks. Because I know who I am. And when I hear the noise, that is enough.

The moneyed have always taken the high ground . . . a story as old as the Greeks. The moneyed have always taken the hilltops, the most visible locations, the shiniest toys. Grass-roots reality isn't interesting to them. I think of the episode of *Downton Abbey* where the Dowager Countess always wins the Gold Cup in the village flower show even though it is her gardener who does all the work. She wants the trophy, not the dirt under her fingernails. And so, on social media, those rich in followers with the luxury of a photographer to follow them around latch on to that which is the most romantic, the most glittery, the gold cup of visibility. We could call it cultural appropriation, but then again, it might be cultural appreciation, and it has nothing to do with me. I've been cashing ranch paychecks my whole adult life, in one form or another, cultivating hard-won skills and getting it done, daily, weekly, monthly, as the seasons come and go and turn into years . . . and more years.

Yesterday I turned down a chance to be on RFD-TV and The Cowboy Channel because the logistics of getting a camera crew that far into the backcountry are too complicated, not to mention scheduling, since weather and animals dictate when we will be where. Today we turn our energy and focus to outfitting camps, ordering vaccine, shoeing up, preparing to move cows and brand calves and sleep on the ground and work from sunup to sundown while I add to a manuscript that is rooted and grounded in my work. That work is in no way threatened by someone else's art—or—and this may be more important—someone else's opinion. And so, no cheers, no flags, no crowds, no glitter, no comment, no critique, my identity rooted in the work, the blood on my chaps, the wear on my saddle, my spurs on my boots that rest in the saddle house and never see the stage or pavement, the soot on my hat, the skills and determination that I am so fucking proud of.

I have dirt under my fingernails.

SPEECH AND DRAMA

Shall we gather at the river, the beautiful, the beautiful river . . .

Centipedes can swim. So can Gila monsters. I know because I saw one playing in the water. I live where there are Gila monsters, and I can introduce you.

The first time I saw the swimming hole was on my very first backpacking trip, late in the second day. We had borrowed backpacking gear and had no idea that we would learn to see this ranch differently. The hike was peopled with all men—Gail and two Game and Fish employees—and me. We stood on the sand and discussed the possibility of climbing around the long stretch of dark water filling the bottom of the canyon. Gail had been in this spot before, but always horseback, never going up canyon, and had never needed to find a way around. The men dropped their packs and talked. They searched for a way forward. Surely this hairy slot of canyon would open and up and show them the way around, allow them entrance. I had neither voice nor vote. After all, I had never been here before either. I would go where they led.

The stained-glass lamp, ornamented with dragonflies, glows softly in my office. I sit beside my grandson's cot, the door to our bedroom open so he will be able to see us in the night. I promise him I will sit with him until he is asleep. It only takes about five minutes, the same amount of time it takes me to scroll through my Instagram feed until it says, "You are all caught up!" We had a busy day. I promise Clint, even as his lashes droop to his cheeks, "If you need me in the night, I am right here."

"When Amy was a baby, if she started to cry in her crib after we put her to bed, I would just yell, *He-Yaw!* and she would stop, just like that, every time."

My father's harsh yell, one that makes my insides clench even now, was the same as the one he used to make the horses stop fighting at graining time or to discipline a naughty dog. He gets a huge laugh out of telling this story. He thought that was what parenting looked like. He thought that was the right way to teach me to go to sleep. I lie still in the dark of adulthood and think of other ways.

Grampa Gail didn't wake Clint when he rose in the dawn to feed horses and make coffee. Clint ran a low-grade fever the night before and Mamie and Grampa thought perhaps he needed his sleep. We whispered about it before Gail rose from our bed, and Grampa tiptoed by the cot, committing the cardinal sin of leaving the boy behind. Mamie did some fast talking and fast hunting up of small jeans and boots when Clint woke ten minutes later, immediately demanding to know where his grampa was.

I stand with my coffee cup and watch from the window as the three-year-old walks through the cold morning, Carhartt coat zipped to his chin, making his way alone, a heartbreaking and yet affirming little figure, going where he wants so desperately to go. I am flooded with the memory of my own short legs carrying me to the barn, only it was afternoon, not morning, West Texas, not Arizona. And I didn't walk toward a grampa who would look up with delight on his face, delighted that Clint walked all that way through the dawn to be with him, a man who will greet him with a familiar joke that will delight the boy.

The joke began several months before when Clint came to stay with us for a week while his mother packed up their house to move from a mining town to the ranch where my son, Oscar, had taken a new job. Less than twenty-four hours after the boy went back to be with his parents, my daughter-in-law, Breanna, called to say that Oscar was having severe abdominal pains, and she was taking him, as fast as she could, to the emergency room. Could we please come get Clint?

In a strange late-evening exchange, Gail and I took her son away as he sobbed in the car seat after a long day with too much sugar and too much scary excitement. He came with us to be lovingly cared for while she stayed with my hurting boy who was being prepped for a middle-of-the-night appendectomy. Breanna cried. I cried. We felt as if our hearts were doing the splits. How could she send her boy off with me? How could I leave my very sick hurting son behind, the one I grew under my heart? It seemed all wrong, and yet, it was exactly right.

Clint was asleep before Gail could drive out of the hospital parking lot.

The next morning, when Gail walked through my office on his way to the bathroom, he looked over at Clint in the blue sleeping bag and saw the wide-open blue eyes. He said, "You again!" Delighted giggles at the joke filled our morning.

It is this man and this joke that my grandson trudges that long way to the barn to find. A joke that never grows old. "You again!" The smell of alfalfa. Rowdy dogs. Meaningful work. A grampa who promises eggs and bacon and a toasted English muffin upon their return to the warm house. And, of course, he will put honey on it.

My memory of walking to the barn is different, but it floods over me as I stand with my coffee and watch that sturdy little back, certain of what he is going to find. The bacon is already in the pan, sending sizzle and scent into the air. I don't hear "You again!" but whap, whap, whap!

When I was three years old, my dad and my grandfather owned a red roan horse named Shorty. He was gentle enough for kids but also good for the men to ride, gathering cattle or roping in the arena. In the house, Mom was folding clean cloth diapers and doing dishes and nursing my baby sister. I walked through the hot afternoon sun because the cool stuff happened at the barn and I could hear the whap, whap, whap of the shoeing hammer as my dad shod a horse. I don't know how it came about, on that afternoon, that my dad let me ride. I remember that he saddled Shorty with my Mexico-built kid saddle Papa bought at a horse sale. He threw me up and told me to ride down the road to the cattle guard on the highway and back. I don't know how far that was, and as I reconstruct early memories, I am loath to ask because the answers don't often mesh with what my tiny child memory stored. In my mind, it was a very long way.

When I see photos of myself at that age, I am not surprised that Shorty wouldn't go. I didn't grow much until I was eleven, so at three I was very small. On the ranch today, I ride a big white horse named Roscoe and I have a hard time being authoritative with my legs. It feels like they stick out perpendicular to my body because he is so round and so big. Could Shorty not feel me kicking him as per my father's instructions shouted from in front of the barn door where his shoeing tools lay scattered in the dirt? Was Shorty reluctant to take orders from a fairy sprite or was I scared to ride all the way to the highway and transmitted that reluctance to the wise cow horse in every way?

What is not a question in my memory is the anger, the eruption and flare of red-hot anger. Dad jerked me off the horse, managed to crawl up into the tiny black saddle gripping a short piece of 2x4. He reined Shorty around and around in a circle while he paddled his ass with the flat of that board. I can still hear *whap whap whap*. Then, he threw me back up into the saddle.

My arm still aches.

He told me to show that horse who was boss and make him walk. All instructions from my father were delivered at high volume, so I could hear them, of course. So that he would be heard. I was sobbing, blinded by tears, and scared. The last thing I wanted to do, now, was ride a horse. But I was and am that infant in her crib in the dark going silent at the sound of her father's voice hollering from the living room.

Shorty was now perfectly willing to walk down the dirt road, maybe, like me, desperate to escape the fury and the frustration that was that man. I rode until the barn was out of sight and sat still for a long time before reining in a large slow circle back. I did not go all the way to the highway.

I am married to a man who can track cattle for long distances through the boulders. I wonder if my father knew that Shorty and I disobeyed him. Did he ever see our tracks?

When Gail and I first got together, we sat over a meal with a woman I had known since I was born, a woman who had always been angry. Time had softened that anger along with her face and her hands and her voice. She spoke of anger and said, "It just hurts you." She is gone now, but just as Clint and Gail have their little joke, so we bounce off that wise old woman's words.

It just hurts you.

♦

I began having panic attacks in sixth grade, every day, second period. The counselor called my mother every morning and she finally stopped coming to the school. All I could feel, see, and understand was the panic.

My happy place was with Mrs. Webb. Mrs. Webb was exotic and when people called me weird, I felt comforted because she was weird, too. She was Native American . . . or half, anyway, half Irish and half Apache, while I was boring and conventional. She wore fringed leather skirts and heavy turquoise jewelry with her long black hair braided down her back. She was a splash of color in what had been, up until then, my very prosaic life. She wore beaded moccasins, laced to her knees. Her home was decorated with furs and leather and stones, sand colors and pale backdrops for elegant pottery curves, not Ethan Allen dark wood conventional that looked like the Sears catalog with sharp corners and straight lines. One of the most striking things about Mrs. Webb was that she was so far removed from the other women I knew. She was childless, the first childless woman my mother's age I had ever encountered.

Mrs. Webb was the junior high speech and drama teacher. Because of her class, listed on my printed schedule, tucked inside the clear front of my notebook, I thought those two words always went together. Speech and drama. It was the first time I had experienced theater or public speaking other than in church.

I found out very quickly that she was already friends with my mother. We had moved back to Fort Stockton, my parents' hometown. Mrs. Webb, or Fredda as my parents called her, had been the maid of honor in my mother's wedding, and my mother would have been in her wedding, except I was born on her wedding day. We repeat the details of story until they are poems we have memorized. I felt immediately robbed of someone I wanted to be my friend; she was already taken by my mother.

And then there was the drama to go with the speech. In the middle of my seventh-grade year, her husband, an old friend of my father's, cheated on her and brought home a disease. It was a horrible scandal that was impossible to keep secret because her students had to get gamma globulin shots, me included. My mother pursed her lips tightly while we were in the pediatrician's office. Fredda's husband met the woman he cheated with at a bar, a detail my mother made sound worse than the disease. Insert horrified gasp.

But Fredda was my friend, a poem of a woman I wanted to memorize. She was both my safe place and my dramatic place. The place

I got straight A's without trying, and I carry a piece of Mrs. Webb every time I go on stage to present spoken word. Now I wish I knew her story of those years, those years of hepatitis and small-town gossip and befriending an adolescent girl with panic attacks.

I don't like loud noises. I perform on stage often, but the idea of going to sound check before any event makes me anxious. I want to duck and run at the first indication of squawk and screech of feedback. I don't like the air compressor at the barn or the old tractor that backfires in low gear or superstores full of sensory overload and intercoms continuously calling for an additional cashier or bombarding me with specials on aisle 9. When we are working cows, sleeping in camp, I would rather go through the tedium and work and waiting of building a wood fire than listen to the noise of a camp stove with propane canister. While I love music, it is superb lyrics that rock me.

I turn everything off when I write and hike so that the words don't get mixed up with the songs and the steps.

A little girl sits on a blonde piano bench in a brick house on 8th Street in a West Texas oil and gas town. As with all towns in that region, oil and gas are looked upon as the necessary but vaguely crass newcomers, while water and agriculture are cloaked with dignity and prestige. In the café on the edge of town, livestock men drink coffee side by side with their greasy counterparts, sometimes switching groups with the season and the day.

The little girl, already in junior high, looks younger than she is, but she has always been small for her age, and her feet dangle above the pedals. Her hands are on the keys, and she knows to pretend that there is a bubble in both palms. Correct technique to make up for lack of musical ability. She is learning a new song from the pages of an exercise book. "Carry Me Back to Ol' Virginny." Piano practice is monotonous, and she stumbles each time in the same place.

Her father sits in his recliner smelling faintly of the oil and gas lease he monitored that day, his boots, spurs, saddle, and horseshoeing tools stowed away in the garage. The oil boom is on. Her piano practice interrupts his reading as the girl stumbles and fumbles with the notes. Irritated, he begins to sing the words to the familiar spiritual. His singing doesn't help. He begins to mock her, laughing loudly each time she hits a wrong note, all bubbles popped, berating her, though in a joking tone, until she is in tears. Doesn't she understand that he is only teasing? She learns that men may say anything they like as long as they smile and laugh as they belittle. He labels her sensitive as the tears run down her face.

Again! he orders. She is no longer bored. She is scared and anxious, determined to get it right and escape the yelling of the man who has never played a note on a musical instrument in his life.

Many years later, the small blonde girl will carry echoes of that day and that song, of his mocking and his frustration. She will wonder, not about the child, but about the man, and what inside of him felt trapped and irritated by thirty minutes of piano practice after school. What dissatisfaction within him overrode lovingkindness?

The little girl may carry an echo, but she is strong, resilient, and watching. She may be carried back in time by melody and memory and male anger, but she stands firm in the present, healed and healing.

It just hurts you . . . unless it also hurts everyone else.

I am creating an anger-free zone. No political or social rants, no rehashing of past wrongs, no lashing out. Angry people must exit the sacred, peaceful, beautiful space and take their fumes of dissatisfaction and putrid toxicity outside where it can dissipate, be filtered by the Mother's breaths so that the energy might escape on the wind.

♦

I married a soft-spoken man who ducks his head and turns away when he says something important or makes a joke. "You again!" He wears a headset mic when he sings onstage so he can't run from it. But in areas where we are the most confident, we don't need a mic. Horseback, working cows, he yells. We don't usually yell at cows much because in this country we need them to be gentle, but the moment he starts yelling at me, I feel my insides clench shut. After all, I am doing my very best. I am not a shirker. There has never been a day in my life that I wasn't doing my best. I want this job to get done as much as he does, and I am doing everything I know to make a hand. I will never be the cowboy that he is, but I am trying harder than anyone he has ever hired. For years I have tensed my whole body against his raised voice, his tone, even his tendency to roll his eyes in disgust when I am not in exactly the right place, at exactly the right angle. Only a few times have I stood up to him, and then only when I can't take it anymore. I have threatened to ride home, and did once, even though he was on a young horse that didn't want to be left alone.

Gail is one of the kindest men I know, but when his blood pressure rises, he turns into the red-faced, spitting-venom man who raised him. We both understand genetics and conditioning. I have my own default when I feel criticized or trapped: a panic attack or temper tantrum; at least it relieves the inner tension.

Recently we were trying to get some gentle slow-moving cows through a gate. We had a time crunch and things got tense. He got loud, and his gestures got big, and I imitated him for the sake of doing the job. I have learned how to get my energy up. When the lead cow walked through and onto the trail, with the rest following behind in a mellow line, Gail paused and softened his voice as he leaned over to stroke his mare on the neck with a soothing gesture. She can be high-strung, so much so that she has stomach ulcers.

"Just theater, Birdie. Just theater. I didn't mean it."

I sat stunned, almost in tears. First came the longing to be that mare, for him to care for me the way he cares for that horse between his knees. Care for me enough to soothe me after a big explosion. Then his words penetrated my held-back tears.

For years I have tensed up my chest and my stomach when he raises his voice. For years I have failed to recognize that sometimes his yelling is simply theater, not a temper tantrum, not anger. The relief that flooded over me was temporary because I have been conditioned from the crib.

Perhaps I am not bipolar. Perhaps I am just angry.

Perhaps it is all just speech and drama.

The leader of that first hike finally made a decision. "The best way to get across is to inflate our sleeping pads, fold them in half, and float our packs." The men continued discussing and pondering and planning. I flipped open the clips that held my rolled sleeping pad, borrowed, from the borrowed pack, stripped off my clothing except for sports bra and panties, and stuffed everything in my pack. I waded out into the water, balanced that borrowed pack on that borrowed sleeping pad and struck out across the deep, dark water, kicking hard.

I didn't want any fucking help.

This was 80 yards of my life I knew I had to do on my own. I was first to reach the far side, first to get dressed again, first to stand and hoist my pack in the evening air.

I have done that swim many times now, sometimes with a 99-cent child's inflatable pool float as a bubble to boost my confidence. Who wants to end up in the middle of the wilderness, naked, no shoes, with their pack at the bottom of the drink?

I own my own gear now, really nice backpacking gear, and no longer have to borrow. And I have come to love backpacking. I hike down here on "my" loop, a hard loop, at least once a year. I know how to do this, and I kick across, the whole world be damned. This is where I belong. This is where I rock life. This is my place. Here is where I shine.

There is no drama here. Just water. Every year I stand on the far shore, nude, my pack safely pulled up into the reeds and grass of the rocky bank.

There is no drama here. But there is also no separation. My pack in the weeds is the only thing marking me apart from this place where I stand, folded into Mother's embrace by rock and water and cactus rising above me into the sky. There is no speech, no human ears to hear my story, no labels to say that I am part of those who are raping and pillaging this planet, that I belong to this group or that. Rather, I stand, toes in the mud, water mid-shin, and face the expanse I have just come through, the water in which I have willingly been immersed, my ritual baptism. The canyon whispers, "You again." I have reached the other side.

There were so many things in my upbringing that were forbidden. I wish I had taken my own children skinny-dipping.

I have another two or so hours of walking with my shell on my back until I might make my nest for the night. But clocks and calendars and borders and maps are arbitrary here. As Wendell Berry says, *I feel above me the day-blind stars waiting with their light.*

Because I can, I walk back into the water where the fish swim along the bottom. The water lifts my breasts. As I go deeper, the wings that sprouted between my shoulder blades during my early morning yoga poses return. In this place, I am a child who can fly. I duck beneath the surface and sink to the bottom.

Bubbles slowly escape from my nose and my hair rises upward from my scalp.

No one cries underwater.

... in the beautiful, the beautiful river ...

THE WINE MULE

for Nick and Artie

This ranch headquarters is nestled in a big boulder pile. Until a few years ago and the emergence of Elon Musk's Starlink, our internet connection was very slow and our data was metered. While everyone else was streaming music and watching Netflix, we cradled our cell phones on signal boosters hoping to have a conversation without dropping the call. We read a lot of books. I stood by the pine tree at the corner of the barn for Zoom calls with my siblings, the only place to get 4G. Even now, when we leave headquarters to work cows, we have zero connectivity for days on end. Gail's autoreply on his email says, "Off in the boondocks, chasing cows. Will reply when we get back to civilization." When I try to explain our connectivity limitations, I always think of a woman I met once, a very successful woman from the Bay Area.

She sat in a camp chair and cried.

She showed up to breakfast at the pack station on the eastern slope of the Sierra Nevada mountains with her cell phone in hand, raising her arm to catch a signal, pulling her text messages from the air. I was one of the guides and the head cook for the backcountry traveling trips out of this pack station, a job I held for two seasons before I came to work on Spider Ranch in 2008, before I came to be with Gail, while I was still married to my first husband, Nick.

I checked her name off the list on the clipboard. "If you will take your duffel to those men there by the pack dock, they will make sure it gets to camp with us. Then, park your car next to the blue one, hang your keys here on the peg board. I have a cup of coffee with your name on it!"

"I have a conference call at eleven. Will that be possible?"

It wasn't until later, on the trail, that I learned more. She hadn't purchased this high-end seven-day traveling pack trip, one the website advertised as "luxury" and "gourmet." She had not chosen five days of constant motion with two layover days beside spectacular lakes in northern Yosemite, six nights in the backcountry, supported by mule teams and guides and a cook. She had won this trip from her boss for being one of the most productive employees on his team. The guests could either hike from camp to camp or ride a horse, a choice to be made upon purchase. But she hadn't made any choices. The whole package was handed to her, a prize won, accepted, and now as real as the horse between her knees. Pack trips into the wilderness, especially those that last seven days, are not about productivity. They are not about connectivity.

From the back of a bay horse named Mack, two miles into the week, she informed me that she also had a conference call three days hence. I laughed. "No, you don't. Not unless you have a satellite phone!"

On a high pass, eleven thousand three hundred feet above sea level, I helped the guests dismount to stretch their legs and drink in the two views at our feet. One showed where we had come from. The other showed where we were going. We marveled at how breathless we were at this elevation, both from the panorama and from the atmosphere. The woman who had won this trip through dedication to her work was not looking at the views. She was standing off to the side looking at the ground, device in hand, alerting her assistant of her imminent lack of connectivity. The moment we dropped over the next ridge, her cell phone would be useless as anything more than a camera, and then only as long as the battery lasted.

When we rode into that first camp, my packers were already busy unloading the mules, my kitchen lying in the dirt by the fire ring, tents and chairs stacked under trees. I handed my horse off to one of the packers and helped the guests dismount. I set my crew to erecting tents and gathering wood for the fire while the guests picked through the duffels.

"Um, excuse me. I was wondering about the facilities." I turned from screwing legs into a camp table to hand the woman who had won the trip a shovel and explain about burning her toilet paper and going downstream from camp.

She sat in a chair and cried. Cried because she was missing her conference calls. Cried because she had to poop and pee in the bushes, downstream. Cried because there were no cabins. "But I brought a hair dryer!" She cried because, I can see now, from the distance of years, she was lost, lost in that place, lost without her connectivity, connection to all that was real to her.

I had a kitchen to set up, a meal to prepare for sixteen people in the backcountry and the word "gourmet" constantly echoing in my head. Back then, I hadn't lost enough to know how to comfort her. Or even deal with her.

My then-husband, a giant of a man named Nick, walked back from the mule line and into camp, coming up behind me to lift the heavy kitchen boxes so I could fit metal legs onto them. In answer to the question on his face, I took him off to the side to explain.

Nick knelt beside that crying woman there in the wilderness. He asked for her help. He explained that along on this trip was an elderly mule named Artie, the smallest mule in the remuda, and that while Artie would normally be in retirement, it made him very sad to get left behind because Artie loved his work. The owner of the pack station often sent him on trips to keep him from being depressed. The only thing Artie carried was wine, so his load got lighter and lighter each evening until by the last day, his pack contained only sacks of garbage. Nick also explained that Artie loved people and sometimes the other mules were mean to him so could she come and help out over at the picket lines? Nick would introduce her to Artie.

That little old wine mule never had it so good. From then on, the woman's horse, Mack, got tied into the pack string in Artie's place. Artie's new friend and caretaker walked from campsite to campsite, leading him every step of that traveling trip. She staked him closer to camp than the other mules and moved him when she decided the grass was too short. She set her chair out beside him on our layover days and they had long conversations. She scratched his ears and led him to water for one last drink each night before she crawled into her tent. Not only did she have a job to do, she had a living, breathing, stubborn little reason to do it.

She cried the first day of the trip, and on the last night, as we sat around the fire, she cried again. She cried because the trip was over. Cried because she had to go back to the city and work and conference calls. Cried because she was going to miss Artie. She cried because unconnected, out there in the wilderness, she found a connection she'd never known before.

IN HEAT

I f I posted scenes from my office today, I'd get banned from social media. Swinging dicks with red-tipped erections. White semen drips and smears. Scuffle and bump and mounting and humping.

Both of my jobs, author and cowboy, may be perceived as glamorous but neither is as romantic as it sounds. The traditional image of the cowboy is often overlaid by a bucolic and pastoral filter. Rarely does one discuss the unspeakable in conjunction with the glossed-over icon that is cowboy, often shown in the arena engaging in sport and wearing a fancy costume rather than doing the down and dirty work of growing food on untillable soil with little to no inputs. On television, ranching is portrayed with helicopters and SUVs and oil wells and lush valleys and expensive clothes; all the animals are fat and sleek. The myth of cowboy shown in photographs or on film is often overlaid with an idealized and romanticized view of our actual work. Rarely do the movies show the miles or the sweat or the days when nothing goes right, and it costs us four days to make up for one mistake. And even with photos posted, the reality is lost in translation. What I am witnessing here in the back of this long line of cattle today is a far cry from the bucolic, the pastoral, a long way from idealistic and romantic.

I often share cell phone pictures of my days, my ever-changing, variable work, a dynamic that those of us in agriculture know well. Although I always "work from home," I generally don't get to stay in my soft clothes or go around barefoot, third cup of coffee in hand, and my office changes with the task. On one day it may be the deep dense green of the creek bottom with baby frogs trying out new legs. On another it may be high up on an arid ridge with an eagle giving me news on the wind. On another, I find a bear track, twice the size of my hand, in the mud of a dirt tank after riding for four hours, more hours horseback to go. Or I may post a photo of my actual office . . . a jungle of house plants with the warm glow of a radiant heater and a dog taking advantage of my good graces, stacks of books and a corkboard full of writing topics in bad handwriting.

But today, my office is astride a horse, in a handmade saddle that fits me better than any desk chair. Gail has split the herd, taking a bite from the first third of the cows we are moving so that he can control the leaders. I have with me, here in the back of the herd, a heifer that smells good. She must smell *great*, as evidenced by the obscene porno I am witnessing. A cow's estrus cycle is not seasonal but rather dictated more by nutrition, gestation, and lactation. She comes on heat every twenty-one days on average, and ruttishness (yes, that is a real word) lasts from three to twenty-four hours.

When we make a cow drive, I always come last. Perhaps one of the biggest compliments of my life arrived a few years ago when a cowboy we hired to help for a few days offered to ride drag. Gail said, "No, I like Amy to come last. I trust her to bring the tiny babies and the grandmas. I trust her not to leave anything behind unless it is completely necessary." And usually, he is right; I come along in the rear with the nursery bunch, with the tired babies who want to lie down in the shade and take a nap . . . easy to ride right by one if mama and I are not paying attention. Also in the back, I often have the old grandmas, the cows who know this country better than we do and understand how to slip away from the herd and stick their heads in a sumac tree to hide instead of going along to the next pasture.

Bulls are territorial and motivated by hormones. When we are cleaning up the left-behind remnant in a pasture, we often gather a disproportionate number of bulls because at the beginning, when we find the big end of these cows on the first jerk, when we have the bigger numbers, it is too easy, when a bull is giving us problems, to say, "Just drop him. We will get him next go-round."

Today our ratio of cows to bulls, which we normally try to keep at ten to one, is lopsided. I have five bulls in the back with me, all of them sniffing and fucking this one heifer who is in heat. We say she is "bulling." But from what I observe she is totally over these bulls. I would be. So much for the bucolic pastoral life. Instead of being in the back with the photogenic wobble-legged nursery cuteness, I am witness to more of a brothel or an orgy, except no one is having much fun. I don't pull my phone out to snap a picture of on-display swinging erections and semen dripping all over the trail, a portrait of aggression, hormones, and fatigue. I only hope we can get where we are going before the heifer is injured. Without our interference, she, first of all, would not be around so many bulls at once, and secondly, would, smart woman that she is, probably run off into the trees and lie down under good cover when she got tired of them.

Consensual sex is a human construct. Hens don't welcome daily copulation with the rooster. Equine copulation is loud and violent. Most mammalian copulation is driven by smell and smell alone, much as I witnessed this morning when the bulls were running to sniff the urine of any cow who spread her legs to pee while eating hay at dawn. The bulls stick their noses into the stream and then lift their top lips in an eeewwww response. They are doing research, a calculation, judging if the time is right to mount a cow and make a calf. She isn't winking at him, saying, "Come on, big boy." She just smells right. What humans deem rape is everywhere in the natural world.

I'm a country girl who thinks sex should be simple. You're cute; I'm horny; let's dance to King George, 'round and 'round in a two-step until we go out in the parking lot and my dad will kill you, cut your thing off, if I get pregnant. If only sex were that simple. Life, since I was old enough to kiss the wrong boy, has been proving

73

my theory wrong. Sex is anything but simple, and the natural world brings it even more into focus.

The mare and I follow along behind the last in this line, a young bull who is not getting his share of the action, semen and manure marking the trail in front of us. The heifer is raw and bleeding by the time we get to the corrals. No matter our past, or what triggers us, or how we view the natural world versus the way humans behave, no matter our traumas or the dense blackness of memory, we live in this moment . . . and our job is to care for those who have less power, less voice. Our responsibility is to the *right here, right now* present reality. I can't make a very big difference, but I can make a small difference.

Gail is waiting to close the gate behind me as we go through into the lot. Perhaps, in the explaining, my voice is a little shrill. Perhaps my emotions spill over. But he honors my request to remove the heifer from the herd, cut her out and put her through the fence ahead of the rest while we finish up the work. It is a financial and managerial decision for him, if not for me.

I sit grateful as the little heifer walks out into the trees alone.

HOUSE OF FEAR

Laestrygonians, Cyclops,
wild Poseidon—you won't encounter them
unless you bring them along inside your soul,
unless your soul sets them up in front of you.
                                    —"Ithaca," C. P. Cavafy

S everal years ago, I was invited to participate in an event
for The Moth, a nonprofit group based in New York City
dedicated to the art and craft of storytelling. For weeks I
rehearsed my story for the producer, on the page, on the phone,
and then in person. No matter how many times I told my story,
she didn't get it.

I told of realizing very soon after I came here to this ranch to be
with Gail that he is an excellent tracker. He can read whole stories
in the dirt. This is rough country. We don't just ride out and find the
cows standing there. Each pasture is several square miles of steep
rocky brushy terrain. Since he had forty-odd years of experience
in looking at the ground, I would put my horse in behind his and
not really go to work until he trailed up the cows. I would look for
arrowheads, identify different birds flitting through the trees, write
pretty poems in my head. Until one day. We saddled up early and I
was riding behind him to Queens and Spades, a pair of dirt tanks

up on a mesa, when he turned and said, "Do you think we are going to jump that bear off the water?" Biting my tongue, I looked down. Right there in the cow trail in front of me was a smoking hot bear track. And I vowed that would never happen to me again. I would learn to see. I would learn to do this job. I would learn to be a valuable member of this team. I would be fully present to this life.

But every time I told the story, the producer from The Moth would explain to me that my fear of the bear wasn't coming through. No matter how many times I tried to tell her that I wasn't scared of the bear, she couldn't hear me. In her mind *I* should have been scared of the bear because *she* was scared of the bear and she couldn't imagine it any other way. She couldn't understand that, for me, being mediocre is way scarier than a bear. She couldn't imagine wanting to learn to do this job that I love. Though I told my story in front of a huge appreciative audience, the recording never made it to the podcast.

Anytime someone hears of my tendency to walk off into the wilderness alone with a pack on my back, they express either fear or longing, though a few quickly dismiss the whole idea as weird and incomprehensible. Most men say something about *be careful* and ask if I go armed. Women often ask, "Aren't you scared?" When prompted, they begin to list the scary things: bears, mountain lions, snakes, coyotes, scorpions. Some of them do not have the nouns at the ready, but if I have the patience to walk them through the examination, we end up at concepts rather than creatures with more or fewer legs than us. We end up at *alone* and *wild* and *space* and *lost* and well, *alone*. No one to talk to. Nothing to occupy the vast expanses of time that open up before us when there are no screens, no newsfeed, no social morass, no list of tasks that must be done, no duty or obligation, nothing calling our names. We end up at facing our selves with no noise to drown out the truth of who we are.

Some women ask, with true terror, about bears and menstruation, about sleeping in the wilderness while bleeding.

It is a legitimate question because we have faced, all our lives, the stigma that comes with the processes of our own biology. We have washed and glossed everything of the natural body.

The most effective method of locking a woman safely away, to keep her from spending time in the wild with the Mother, is to make her feel unsafe because of menstruation. Most women, between puberty and menopause, live through the life/death/life cycle every four weeks unless it has been cut or medicated away. This cycle has been used to make her feel both dirty and unsafe, every four weeks. "Sanitary" products imply that that which issues from her body is not clean. The word "tampon" comes from the French word for "plug" or "stopper." Stop her from sleeping under the stars in the wild by implying that her menses make her unsafe.

The wild animals will devour her.

What is more true is that the wild will devour her, will devour her oldness, her staleness, her fear, her foggy stifled way of being in her world of duty and obligation, her inertia, her consideration of what anyone else thinks.

The truth is that menstruation is not bleeding. The issue from her womb is not so much blood but the sloughing off of the lining of the uterus. It is a releasing of all that no longer serves her. But, because it is red and it flows from her body, it has been named such. Yes, menstruation has an odor, but so do excrement and sweat and urine and belching and even breathing. I have worked around some very smelly boys in my life.

And so, once again, our femaleness has been used to put us in our place, within walls and forts, held down and back and in, so that we don't run off into the woods, the pagan and glorious wilderness.

Working out of doors has taught me to love and trust my body, the trust more important than the love, just like in a long marriage. I trust my bones and my muscles to carry me, the clothing I choose to protect me. I don't use soap on my skin. I celebrate that the horses I ride are familiar with my smell and add their scent to mine. The cows walk right into camp and stand by my cooking fire, for I have not sprayed away all that is natural. It has been years since I have been stung by a wasp or a bee, for I smell of woman, not flower.

I have a well-worn speech about unsocialized black bears and mountain lions who have gotten a bad rap in the urban/wildlife interface and national parklands. Gail and I tell stories on stage about wild animal behavior in the true wild, the unencroached-upon wild. I have personal stories about encounters with bears. Even more common is for me to see a skunk coming in the night to drink at the pools where I sleep. I'd rather talk about black hawks singing me down the canyon and foxes' mating calls at dusk and the swoop patterns of bats. I have a spoken word poem, a slam piece, that I perform on stage, written after interactions on social media with men who would explain the dangers to the poor girl who might get hurt out there, even as they sit behind screens, only observing. As if I am not surrounded by men in real life who want me to be safe. Or stay home.

Permission granted to stand at my funeral and say I told you so.

The demand for explanation can be exhausting. It has intensified lately after a sixty-four-year-old experienced hiker got lost in our area while I myself was off on one of my own backpacking adventures. I followed the story of his rescue when I returned home, plugged back in. So if a MAN can get lost out there . . .

. . . and it is not worth pulling out the maps and describing my day job, a decade and a half of being horseback for hours and hours, days and days through this country, explaining fence lines and topping out high to see obvious landmarks as recognizable as familiar faces, how all game and cow trails lead to water, and the simple fact that this place is my neighborhood, my backyard. No, it doesn't look like yours. Most of us prefer a landscape labeled and marked with words painted neatly on a sign. Thinking and intimacy are hard and scary. And so, without fear, I curl up in the nest of my own abilities and knowledge. No, I will not scoot over and make room. Go make your own.

Fear is often groundless. My grandson points to the spider in the bathtub, a harvestman, often called a granddaddy longlegs. We have an abundance of them here, even gregarious clusters doing bouncy push-ups in the corners of the woodshed. Clint knows that Mamie and Grampa Gail don't kill things. The urban myth contends that harvestmen are the most venomous animals in the world but that their fangs are not long enough to bite a human. Science, via a quick Google search, slays that urban myth with the information that harvestmen have neither venom glands nor fangs and are not true spiders at all.

I am terrified of my own mediocrity, the seed inside us all that says, "Oh, well. Good enough." I've allowed it to take over previously tended fields like housekeeping and cooking, bringing my full energy to cultivating that which feeds my passion. I write and hike and ride my way through the wild rather than the conventional and over-domesticated. What else am I to do? Stay home and allow middle age to catch up with me and settle around my shoulders?

I fear duty and obligation and love that comes with a price tag.

Some fears we are born with, like my paralysis up on a rooftop and on the ladder leaned against the high stack of hay in the barn and my certainty that while I like air travel, I do not need to jump out of an airplane and float to the ground to be a badass wild woman. I have scared myself enough climbing around in these rocks with the weight of a pack on my back, altering my center of gravity. I have talked myself out of my fear of murky water, one that blossomed in childhood when powerful hands rendered me powerless, swinging me in the air and threatening to throw me into the middle of a muddy stock pond where there was sure to be a "big ol' snapping turtle." Fear even keeps me from being the best horsewoman I could be when I want to step off rather than being alpha.

I fear my tendency to judge another's fear, and I am scared, here in midlife, that someone will ask me to carry their emotions, that I will lead someone off into the wilderness of discomfort. And yet, out of love, I did lead a group of seven women to a camp down below ranch headquarters, close enough that Gail could haul in our gear while we walked the four miles.

I knew their fears. They had, at my invitation, expressed them freely, and I tried ad nauseam to put them to rest. But fear rarely takes a rest and, as Cavafy points out, each of us carries our own monsters within us.

The mosquitoes bowed out for the weekend, and it was a grand adventure. I had prepared all of the camp gear and my full outdoor kitchen, even cooking some meals in advance. The whole experience was ideal.

And even when she showed up, it remained ideal.

In passionate reflection, I realize that there is no better situation than having fear show her face and allow herself to be photographed and documented, so that we can look back on the moment and tell the story.

We sat in a circle through the lazy afternoon of our full day in camp, a true women's circle in the shade, an echo of an ancient pagan drum circle. The talk was gentle and raucous in turn. The breeze cooled the afternoon to just the right degree.

As the conversation swirled, I turned my head, and over my right shoulder, I saw her, long and black and stretched out, not moving. She'd uncoiled from her den in the roots of the juniper on the high creekbank. I said, "I need everyone to get up and move quietly to stand behind Mary's chair." Not everyone did as I asked. I had to change my tone to move those who were less willing to be led. Because one of our number is a brilliant photographer, I asked her to get her camera. I knew of her fear, but I also knew, and never doubted, that her talent and drive would rise above.

The questions began to come fast, like pepper sprinkled through the air, and I saw the paralysis in some eyes. But fear is often still and quiet. The snake, a timber rattler, a species I know to be more docile than the coon-tails or diamondbacks, lay still. She was real, but she was not dangerous. She wouldn't become dangerous unless threatened by her own fear.

Every woman carried home photographs of that beautiful creature. We moved her with a shovel gently out and away from camp, yes, and there was a small drama, enough to make a good story. She finally buzzed, making her own fear audible. Once she had been relocated down the bank toward the creek and out of our space, we moved our chairs to another pool of shade. I thought about her as we sat and picked up the thread of conversation once again.

How rude are we?

We came to her house.

BEAVER AND BALANCE

The whole world's gone crazy, and the sky is falling.
—Mandy Rowden, "Enough for Us All"

My office is a haven of creativity and sanity. On a red trunk, atop a small woven rug, I have created a cairn of stones, picked up on various river trips and hikes. Sometimes the cairn topples over, balance disturbed by a carelessly placed coffee cup or the bump of a broom. Or perhaps, I suspect, by the earth's seismic activity and spinning through space. When I see that the balance has been disturbed, I stop and restack the stones. Sometimes this is easy. But on some days, I must pause, breathe, sit down—on the floor even—calm myself. Bring myself into balance before the rocks will cooperate between my fingers.

I am not a biologist, just a middle-aged nature lover who has hiked a long way from a cow camp up higher on the rim to sit here, at the confluence of two canyons, beside the remnants of a beaver dam to try and make sense of a world gone crazy. When I discovered that beaver had returned to our watershed, Gail was just as excited as I was. I called our Game and Fish Wildlife Manager with caution because the management of resources on public land is a delicate balance. When I told him I had just returned from backpacking a loop he is familiar with, he asked, "How was it?"

"Great! I will lose some toenails, but . . ."

"Yeah," he said, "that's why I'm not hiking down there ever again."

"So, that place where we have to swim? Where there is no way around? It is quite a bit longer . . ."

"Why? Got a beaver? I've been expecting them to show up there someday."

But then, the fire came, a managed disaster, a lightning strike the Forest Service turned into a rangeland management event. I stood in a crowd of men who spoke of "dropping fire," and, working to keep my voice from shaking, asked that the beaver dam be listed as a resource to be protected. Please don't drop fire there.

In the aftermath, we faced the impossible task of gathering the cows back up with cut fences and down water gaps, no time for sleeping on a rocky creekbank for the pleasure of viewing wildlife. Our busy autumn was followed by a very wet winter beginning with a Thanksgiving meal shared on a Wednesday, a decision precipitated by the storm forecast. Our Black Friday was pristine white and snowed in, no electricity, and two very understanding houseguests. We drank hot tea and ate food reheated on the woodstove. Bucolic and idyllic and postcard-beautiful until the thaw revealed our forest and fences devastated with downed branches, grandmother oaks destroyed, uprooted sycamores in the creeks.

The storms kept on coming, blessed moisture, but from a distance, I kept imagining the burn scar, topsoil washing down the slopes, down the canyons, floods carrying black soot into every pool and washing out the beaver's brand-new dam.

The year 2020 dawned. And the Great Mother shrugged. She shrugged her shoulders, ridding herself of a few of the biting drilling parasites she's carried for so long. No matter our screaming and scheming, our population is too dense. We do not get to choose who is removed. The Great Mother is tired of us, and this is our doing.

I turned fifty years old during a pandemic, a statement that seemed important to note until everyone who stayed alive had a birthday overshadowed by COVID-19, and then another. My husband graciously joined me on a day hike, and, that night, cooked steaks. He ordered me a new headlamp from Amazon. We played a game of cribbage. He won.

So much for the privilege of going out to eat and clinking bar glasses, our meal cooked by someone else and delivered to the table, beautifully plated. Those luxuries were for another time and seem trivial in light of the circumstances.

My real birthday gift came thirty days later. We went on my dream hike, the one it is unsafe to attempt solo, the one he had promised me for so long. I estimated that the route would take at least five days, and toward the end of our planning, we decided we might be able to do it in four. It took six. Six very hard long days. Five nights sleeping in the bottoms of the canyons. Six full days unplugged, no awareness of the climbing numbers, the graphs, the reports, the briefings, the deaths, the posturing and politicizing, the divisive rants or gloom-and-doom reports. Clambering through the boulders was an easier course. We were serenely and yet not so serenely oblivious.

Day three kicked my ass.

On day four we finally arrived at the place where I had seen the beaver dam, eager to observe how the beaver had fared through fire and flood. After we swam the deep pool, water from wall to wall of the slot canyon, we stood, drying off and pulling lunch out of our packs, and decided that the floods from the burn scar must have discouraged the beaver. He must have moved on. The biologist I spoke with told me not to be shocked at the seeming devastation in a riparian area with beaver. And indeed, our immigrant worker had created a construction zone with felled willow and ash trees, but we couldn't see the actual structure he had built. As I was finishing my salami and cheese, Gail said, quietly, "There's a beaver." Sure enough, he was checking us out. He swam from under the far bank, made a slow arc in the water, watching us from the corner of his eye. He was not only coming to see who these noisy swimmers were but showing himself to us before he pulled himself up onto what we then saw was the front porch of his home, a slick muddy trail leading into a pile of debris against the opposite canyon wall. He disappeared into his burrow.

Even the hardest times deliver gifts.

For years we have discussed our dream to someday live on a boat or build a home of our own where we would live off-grid in as sustainable a fashion as possible. On this hike, though, the melody changed.

My mother was strict about the language we used as children. We weren't allowed to use the words *luck* or *lucky*. She doesn't believe in luck. She believes the whole world is in God's hands, so we are blessed by Him, but never lucky. Because I talk about my life here on the ranch on stage quite often, and I take a lot of photos that go up on social media, I hear about how "lucky" I am. On long, hot, sweaty, hard days when I am working for wages, that word drives me crazy. Conscious choice and wet saddle blankets got me here. Determination and love help me stay. An old friend likes to say, "The harder I work the luckier I get," so I stole the phrase from him and wrote a slam poem to that effect.

That was before the pandemic. That was before shelter-in-place. That was before we watched jobs and travel plans and businesses disappear beneath the wave of rising numbers. That was before people panicked about toilet paper and their food supply. Now, instead of boat shopping, we keep saying, "Why in the world would we want to be anywhere but here?" We have friends and family, all over the world, trapped in apartments smaller than the flat areas beside the creek where we wriggle our way into the sand, making our beds each night of this hike. We began our sheltering-in-place with freezers full of beef and seeds ready to go into the ground, a henhouse full of layers and a little red hen gone broody. We have meaningful work we love, and our bodies are strong. We don't own one horse or one cow or one acre of land, but we have a lot of horses and cows and so much room to roam. We don't punch a time clock, ever. The owners of the ranch shrugged their shoulders when the cow market dipped hard due to a bottleneck at the packing houses, and we didn't ask anyone's permission to walk off, away from headquarters, for this glorious six days. After we left the familiar roads and trails, we saw little evidence of other humans. At that time, the skies were still clear of most air traffic. Even at headquarters we cannot hear street or highway sounds and the sky is unobscured by light pollution. We live at the end of the dirt road, nearest neighbors miles away. Our paychecks are direct-deposited, the Arizona sunsets are spectacular, the electric lights come on with the flip of a switch, and we don't even pay the bills. We have been lovers for almost a dozen years, but now we smile gently at each other, a bear track in the sand beside our bed tonight. We know that we like each other, and that is pretty fucking important.

The night after we saw the beaver, lying side by side in our sleeping bags, the low-hung stars reflected off the water at our feet, Gail murmured, "That was a god moment."

Back at home, while I was trying to write about the pandemic in light of our hike, Gail made a trip to the other side of the ranch on the quad and came back with bad news. Neighbor cows had come through the fence and were on a piece of land we have been working hard to rest, hoping for the recovery of perennial grasses. We mounted a defense with a full camp, a trailer loaded with hay, two horses, a cooler, and a journal tucked in my duffel. The beauty of my two jobs is that they often go hand in hand, and I can help gather cows while writing on soot-smudged pages in the morning, comforted by whiskey and surrounded by pink-drenched skies at night.

The days in camp were long and hot, sometimes hard, but with my ink colored by changed perspective, I wrote about how lucky I am to live here, to do the work I do, to adore the one I am sheltering in place with, and how much I like cows. I am so lucky my teeth hurt.

We rode home to face a world on fire . . . to the brutal truth of George Floyd's murder at the hands of a "peace officer." We came home to a world changed, never to be the same again.

Texas songwriter Mandy Rowden on replay, over and over in my head, "The whole world's gone crazy and the sky is falling . . ."

We sat stunned as wave after wave of information and propaganda rolled in, blinded by the darkness that fully fell on our land.

My pen went silent.

And now, I have taken some days off from my work on the ranch to hike down here where the beaver lives, to sit still and try to make sense of things.

I am not a musician, but I've come to understand the value of a pause.

I am not a historian, but I know we are living through history.

I am not a banker, but I know what abundance looks like.

I am not a grammarian, but I know that possessive pronouns are a problem. I am irritated with the beaver because he has changed my definitions. This pool where I sit is no longer designated as "the swim," because he moved in. It was *my* pond, *my* challenge on a solo backpacking loop that I guard jealously, *my* swim, way before it was his home. For three or four years, a photo of this place has been the lock screen on my phone, swipe to open. Now it is the beaver pond.

He is an immigrant, migrating here to feed what, I suspect, is his growing family.

I am irritated with other changed definitions all around me. I will never again sing along to Lee Greenwood with tears in my voice because I am no longer proud. We shop for groceries differently, going backward in time to plastic bags so as to keep from spreading germs with reusable cloth totes, and my mask phobia seems trivial now, especially since I discovered that it isn't about being able to breathe so much as not being able to see whether someone is smiling or not. My silly life.

It is so much more than irritation, though. The world had front-row seats to the death of a human being, executed on the pavement, and then were made acutely aware of how many silenced names have uttered the same phrase, the simple request for the freedom to breathe.

I am not a physician, but I know life is all about breathing. Our privilege may be measured by how easily we take breathing for granted during these times . . . these times of a pandemic that steals our breath, these times when the color of our skin and location of our neighborhood dictate how we are treated by our fellow man.

Breathing is the true gift. In meditation I touch lightly on the out-breath even though the in-breath is so much more interesting. A friend tells me, when I am seeking a series of yoga poses to help me sleep at night, "Don't forget . . . yoga is not so much about poses as it is breathing."

The fish in the water before me rise to the surface and the tadpoles make O's with their soon-to-be-frog mouths, taking in air. Even the leaves on the trees around me are breathing, stomata exchanging gasses with the atmosphere. The rocks that rise above me are breathing with bacteria. Our first and last breaths should be sacred, and even this one, this breath, this one right here as I sit, gear scattered around me, a blue sarong over my head for shade, this one. It is all I have, and it is precious.

I am not a scholar, but I know that science is pretty damned important.

I am not a cleric, but I know that life is sacred.

I am not a preacher, a pastor, a shepherd leading a flock, but in my heartbreak, I reached out to one such whom I love. We exchange emails, though we acknowledge the differences in our beliefs. I wrote to ask him why it is that not one atheist or agnostic among my friends has posted a single racist or violent meme or comment during this dark time, but the Christians that litter my social media have liked, supported, cheered, shared, and even advocated heinous ideas like "locked and loaded" or "all lives splatter." Yes. Splatter. A cartoon car driving into a cartoon crowd with cartoon people flying through the air. I sobbed in horror that someone who professes to worship the God of Peace would post something like that on a public platform. I asked these questions of my dear friend in what I hoped was an honest, open fashion. His reply, in a series of emails loaded with Bible verses, can be summarized: "The world is a sinful place and I am praying for you."

Our community canceled the Fourth of July parade to encourage further social distancing, but one group decided to parade anyway, waving a flag declaring white supremacy. Prayer will not heal a broken heart. Nor should it.

The pediatrician I took my children to when they were small had a physician's assistant named Berlinda. One hot summer day in the Texas Panhandle, I was frustrated and exhausted from driving a baby and a preschooler eighty miles to the doctor's office, thirty-five of that dirt road. As I sat, nursing my infant while trying to keep my terribly busy boy occupied, Berlinda paused before walking out of the examination room to say, "When a child is fussy, add water. Internal or external. The first chemical the brain releases to indicate dehydration is an anxiety chemical, before our mouths are even dry. That is why we nurse a fussy baby. Not because she is hungry, but because she is thirsty. Just add water. It will help." After she left, she stuck her head back in. "It works with cowboys, too."

Just add water.

I am a flee animal. I have hiked down here to sleep beside the water. I have fled the noise while acknowledging that my freedom and ability, physical and locational, to do so is a true blessing. My coming here silences the newsfeed, but the low desert is loud, even at midday in midsummer. Canyon wrens trilling, flickers fussing up on the slopes, wind, locusts, water lapping against rock, fish jumping to catch a snack, even the damselflies and dragonflies clicking around in the reeds are loud.

My heart is aching and sore. My mind is confused by the darkness of the past weeks, and I don't know right or wrong, or how my voice should sound. And I see my own privilege in having this place, this land to roam, and even this time to ask these questions. There is no healing from the knowledge of brutality, from a pandemic shutting down our world, but there is water. For now. We always hope for monsoon rains in July.

Last night, as we lay in bed in the little cabin that is our second home, that place of no electricity or indoor plumbing, but a place with songs and books and love, I asked, "Have you ever been ashamed of the color of your skin?" And my lover replied there in the darkness, "I am right now."

Oh, how I wish I were a rainbow—or even a black and white dragonfly—all colors and none.

We've taken a knee while the colors fly out of respect for the rights of those who were born the same as us on the inside, but of a different hue on the outside, out of respect for all who have cried out without being heard, for all who have been silenced.

The beaver didn't show himself to me in the evening, after I set up my extremely minimal camp, my back to the stone wall of this canyon.

The beaver didn't show himself to me at dawn, though I rose early and made little motion or noise while building my coffee fire.

At 8 o'clock on one of the most beautiful mornings of my life, I write, "The beaver has no obligation to show himself to me," one of the most arrogant statements of my life. As my pen stopped scratching, I heard a deep, throaty, angry growl. I turned my head toward the sound, confused. Perhaps, I thought, the sound came from a bobcat up on the slope? Or a bear coming up canyon, warning me? I know it wasn't a mountain lion. What it truly sounded like was the growling of a pair of fighting badgers I saw once. Then I realized that it was the beaver, growling from the entrance to his home. He was saying, "Okay, bitch. I stayed hidden all day yesterday and today I'd like to come out and get some work done."

I sat and giggled to myself, still hopeful, still arrogant.

A Hopi chipmunk ran past my feet and paused at the water's edge, tail raised for balance, glanced back over his shoulder, saw me, and dashed away in alarm, not getting the drink he came for.

A few minutes later I heard what sounded like a horse, blowing rollers through its nose, sucking in as much air as possible to get the scent of danger, blowing it out loudly to seem bigger, scarier. I raised my eyes to the cliffs above me. A doe ran among the cactus and catclaw, stopping to stare at me from every shadow, trying to identify this intruder at her watering place.

Sometimes we need our messages in threes.

I am not a peace officer, but I know that my being here for too long is disrupting the peace and balance of this place. It is time for me to go.

Human beings crave closure. We want every essay tied up in a neat nice bow, every book release to elicit glowing reviews. We want the shepherds to keep us safe and our leaders to have answers and comfort. We want every birth to go as planned and every death to be peaceful, with all the right words said and hearts mended. We want easy worship with no hard questions.

We want pandemics to come to decisive ends, cures for all that hurts. We want to vote for the winning team every election year. We want racism to have been over in the decade of peaceful hippies. We want every relationship to be healed and every harvest to be bountiful.

But we do not always get closure. Sometimes we stay at home like we were told and then decide, damn it, we want to go out to eat and for a bartender to serve us drinks and the pandemic doesn't just magically go away with hot weather, vaccines, and time. Sometimes we must put our own accident of birth aside and acknowledge our differences and our sameness under the skin, acknowledge what we've been given through no effort of our own. We sit with it. Sometimes the songs of our childhood continue as background music even when we no longer have faith in the old symbols and myths. And we don't get to decide what we believe, chisel it in stone, and close our minds to all new revelations and shifting information.

We don't always get closure, and even if we do, the story keeps on going. Life is not over with one election, thousands of protesters in hundreds of cities, or yellow letters painted on the street, or two years of pandemic bleeding into the third. More action is needed even when we are tired.

Sometimes we hike a long way for a glimpse of a beaver, for a small bit of magic when our soul longs for it the most and we don't get it. The beaver is under no obligation to show himself to me. The beaver and I don't know if more flood or fire or disruption is coming. I am an optimist, but living in the desert, like living in times of unrest and upheaval, makes a skeptic of even the most hopeful. We'll believe it when we are dumping it out of the rain gauge, no matter what the forecast says. The beaver and I can't predict the monsoons, but we are here, no matter what comes our way.

And though I tuck every tiny scrap of my own garbage in my pack and fully believe in leaving no trace of my presence behind, before I hoist that pack on my back, I pile four small stones into a cairn for the beaver. The spin of the earth or a wild drinker will topple them just as we all topple from time to time. I leave them as a thank-you note.

COOKIES AT THE TOP OF THE WORLD

for Clint Lucas

From a distance, the world looks blue and green
And the snow-capped mountains white.
From a distance, the ocean meets the stream
And the eagle takes to flight.

—Julie Gold, "From a Distance"

T he coffee table in our living room is covered in artifacts lifted from the ground where the ancient lived, in layers, from the most primitive sherds of pottery to the delicate sophistication of the tiniest bird and ceremonial points. Our windowsills are lined with *manos*, or grinding stones. This land has harbored humans for so long. Today, the stout-hearted and able-bodied may climb to the high points in this region to discover ancient ruins, evidence of a communication system I wish I understood. Rock walls and petroglyphs mark where people stood, looking from peak to peak. Many archeologists believe these Indigenous peoples were communicating with each other in some manner. So much has been lost with the winds of time and progress. So much will be lost. In a hundred years, all new people. That brings things into perspective.

Jones Mountain rises high above ranch headquarters, not so much a mountain as a huge pile of boulders haired over with cat-claw, manzanita, oakbrush, piñon pine, Spanish dagger, prickly pear, and juniper. At the top, ancient rock walls run along the rim, invisi-ble from the base with its litter of smashed clay pots. We speculate that the ruin was defensive in nature. A series of cairns, placed by adventurous hikers in the know, are piled carefully to mark what is, by most considerations, the only path to the top. Shifts of the earth and weather topple the cairns from time to time. My grand-son, Clint, is eight now, and we love to fill water bottles and pack a picnic so we might hike to the top of Jones Mountain. After leaving the house, we follow a cow trail past the pond north of the barn and along the fence line until we find the first cairn, a vocabulary word we roll around in our mouths, not one he hears in school. Just a Mamie word.

The rule is that Mamie won't leave one cairn until he spots the next one. Like an Easter egg hunt with challenge and purpose. The truth is that it is a very hard hike . . . no trail, huge boulders, and stickers everywhere. If I ever have to haul a grandkid to the ER for stitches, it will probably be because we were climbing Jones Mountain. Clint loves it, and we re-pile the tumbled stones while discussing the plants and bugs and lizards we find along the way.

Once at the top we exclaim over the view of home at our feet, the cluster of vehicles and buildings like toys. The journey was hard and needs documenting. We take several triumphant pictures. I pull our lunch from my pack.

"Mamie, are you a real grandma?"

This boy makes me pause. He often brings puzzles to Gail and me that we try to help him figure out.

"Well, yes. I am your dad's mother. That makes me your grandmother."

"Noooo, Mamie!" He is frustrated with me and with language. "I mean, are you a *real* grandma?"

"Clint, you are going to have to help me out, explain to me what you are asking."

"Mamie! We just climbed a *mountain*!" His grand gesture encompasses the huge sky and the path we've just navigated. He is asking if I am elderly, asking how to equate the image of *grandmother* he has seen on television—the image of someone old, frail, gray-headed, sedate—with me, this woman who is always taking him on adventures. So, we talk about age and ability, health and fitness.

My vision turns from this blond boy, this piece of my heart floating around outside my body, to look out over this small, but seeming large, piece of the map. Our conversations will grow progressively harder as Clint gets older, and I ache to hold onto this moment, this time when he is still excited about hiking with his grandma and still coming to me with questions I can answer.

I like being way up here on this mountain, looking over this place I call home. This is where I ride, and I know where the cows like to drink, their trails through the boulders, where they bed down. I know the old lion scratch beside the spring and the rocky basin where the holdouts will spend the winter. I know of a waterfall and a bear track and an eagle's nest.

I know how to get around out here, how to survive, how to thrive.

I hand my little man a sandwich and a tangerine. He knows Mamie doesn't buy much sugar, so the cookies I have tucked away for later will be a surprise.

I know the hike back home, and we'll chop vegetables together for spaghetti.

I know how to hang out with little boys, but I don't know how to tell this child how to live in this world, in these times. How to navigate AI and TikTok, the noise, the gunshots, the news, the lies.

Someday I will take him deep into my wilderness and we'll sleep out with the foxes and maverick bulls and canyon wrens. With the noisy frogs and silent lions and midnight skunks coming to drink. We won't need a gun.

Today we sit where the ancient sat, carefully gathering the tangerine peel, no trace of us left behind amongst the traces of this disappeared culture.

If identity is wrapped up in ability, then yes, this Mamie climbed a mountain and next week I'll ride off to do a hard job in this rough land, but oh, my boy, Mamie doesn't have the ability to help you live a life my parents painted as simple.

They were wrong, their prescriptions faulty and misguided.

So, I'll not pretend. I'll not hand you duty and obligation or advice and scripture.

When you get out of the bath tonight, I'll wrap you in a towel, call you my *burrito boy*, but as the months fly by, I know that even these moments are fleeting and soon you won't want toys in the tub or a Mamie in the bathroom. And your beloved grampa will soon put a mark on the door frame, higher than my head, to show how much you've grown.

My father's faulty counsel . . . my grandfather's striving for wealth . . . my mother's dictates around chores and clothing and education . . . they all seem silly up here on this mountaintop.

As do my own rules about sugar.

Have a cookie, kid. I'll have one, too.

MAKE A LITTLE REVOLUTION

The blood of two English teachers runs in my veins, and I love diagramming sentences. Precise lines that take sentences apart and put them back together, the building blocks of language defined.

I like charts and graphs and line drawings that explain things; I am drawn to methods and ways. Someone tell me how to do it and I will do it. When I first encountered Andy Wilkinson's creative process model, I got past the big words and the references to Heidegger simply so I could see if what he had to say would lead me through the dense forest of writing that first book. I embraced the chart, vectors, and cones where one might balance and stay centered on that golden thread of truth. The original diagram, which I saw and began using long before it was included in *Mystery Mechanics: The Creative Process*, is my dance floor, well-polished by my eager pen, and I use that gold thread as my barre, finding balance while diving off into the quadrants. Poetry and science lend themselves to creative nonfiction, and I analyze my way into the synthesis over and over again. I see the beauty in grounding the abstract in the concrete. Preaching the sermon with the perfect detail. Literature, art, music, and the Great Mother come into focus for me, accessible through this lens.

Still, what of the mystery?

When I lead workshops, the participants want me to show them how this writing thing is done, and while I have developed a curriculum of techniques, when it comes to making the words sing and the metaphors merge, I admit that the muse can be a fairy or a troll. Some magic caves must be explored alone.

My friend Stephanie is German, but she lives in France most of the year. She works hard from early spring until the Mediterranean tourist season is over in autumn. Late every October she comes to the States to stay in her condo in Scottsdale. She is usually here four or five days, sometimes a week, before she calls and wants to drive up and work cows with us, no matter that she lives on a ranch in the south of France, managing a *manade*, a herd of cows. No matter that it sounds like a busman's holiday to me. She'll even sleep out at camp with us if I'll throw in a tent for her.

Stephanie is trilingual, and I love the quirky way she uses English. Once, when she was helping us, riding an old gelding named Ivan, she told me that he was *crunchy*. It took me all day to figure out she meant *cranky*. Now she has asked for my help. She says that some women must *make a little revolution*. Her current revolution includes her first tattoo, and I have to acknowledge my own bad influence in the realm of rebellion against antiquated social mores. I am always planning my next tattoo. My daughter says I am not aging so much as becoming an art installation; I'm fine with that.

On a cold December Sunday we found a parking spot and kept our tattoo appointment with plans to, as Stephanie expressed it, *make a little party* afterward.

Stephanie is a very precise person. She wants what she wants. She thinks what she thinks, and she will tell you about it. I am sure that a chart and a graph with vectors would suit her just fine. But tattoo artists are generally more relaxed personalities.

On that December day, I had a front-row seat when *very precise* met *high creative* in a small clash that ended in my tattoo artist kicking us back out into the wind. Her exact words were, "Go away. Go get lunch or go shopping or something while I draw." She needed to focus on her work without distraction. I had to talk Stephanie down from the cliff as we walked over to the coffee shop. Within my own experience were planted seeds of faith . . . faith in the creative process. Faith in my friend and tattoo artist, Kat. Faith in something mysterious that cannot be charted or mapped or diagrammed.

Sometimes we have to leap in with both feet. Sometimes we have to believe.

Back in the basement of the shop, the drawings made, Stephanie and Kat bent their heads over the iPad, shifting and shrinking and altering and discussing the precise placement of each element of a bracelet made of rosary beads, hung with charms meaningful to Stephanie. I wandered around, just as I do out of doors, absorbing the atmosphere and details of that environment. Each tattoo shop, like each artist's studio, like each musician's cave, like each writer's haven, like each woodworker's bench, has its own flavor. This one was full of clichés associated with tattoos: S&M posters in the bathroom, a condom package that read "Because lasers can't remove babies," and a dead cat in a jar perched on a shelf above Kat's guest cubicle.

Finally, after much minute alteration, the stencils were made, expanded and then shrunk, placed, scrubbed away, and refined. And the tattoo, hours later, was perfect. As a surprising finishing touch, at least to me, the nonvisual, Kat added white highlights to the gray and black design so that the fine details popped.

When the session was over and we had taken multiple photos to send to Stephanie's daughter in Spain, Kat turned to me. "Your turn!"

My plan had been to have her alter the two small black butterflies outlined on my collarbone that looked too stark to me. Stark in prose is one thing; stark on my collarbone quite another.

Kat and I know each other well. She is the only one who has ever put ink under my skin. I began to use words, my medium. I spoke of the delicate blue and yellow butterflies in the deep riparian bottoms, the Lepidoptera puddlers that dip feet and proboscises into the muddy verge, declaring the health of the wetlands and making the canyons dance. I used words like watercolor and abstract and "less stark," soft, and delicate. Kat, a fellow hiker and wild woman, caught my enthusiasm. No longer were we discussing a tattoo, but the natural world and the mysterious feeling that comes from oneness and unity with the Mother.

"Do you care if I freehand this?"

Leaping in with both feet, I lay down on the table. Kat pulled out a handful of Sharpie markers and went to work on my skin. I had put my phone aside, but Stephanie stood over me furiously taking myriad pictures, not understanding what was happening. Where was the two-hour discussion of what I wanted? Where was the drawing on the iPad and the purple stencil tweaked centimeter by centimeter? Where was the careful placement? What was all of this orange and teal marker drawn swiftly in an abstract guide directly onto my skin? Her distress was palpable.

Kat looked up from her work. "Why don't you go get some tea and a snack from the café next door?"

After Stephanie left, Kat began to fill ink caps with color, not just blue and yellow, but teal and soft browns and tans, pink and fuchsia. The dead cat and I sensed that something ineffable was about to happen, something of creative process that cannot be fully explained.

Stephanie and I did, indeed, make our little party before driving the long dark road home and retreating to our beds with ginger tea and blueberry scones. The next morning, I had a private reveal in the bathroom mirror. The abstract watercolor aggregation of yellow and blue puddlers is in the running for my favorite tattoo design ever.

I don't know how it happened. Creative energy cannot be bought or sold or defined, just as we don't know how to call in the White Goddess, the poetry myth conjunction of wild place musings. Just as there are moments in art that no one can understand. Just as sometimes we must make a little revolution with Sharpie markers on skin. Just as I will never know how that cat got in that fucking jar.

DOUBLE HELIX

The cardinals are molting in August, here in Central Texas. They flutter at the seed feeder and in the stone basin full of water. A squirrel drops down from the eaves, hanging by his back feet while he steals seed.

On the other side of the house, a garden spider rests in the center of her web, enduring in beauty through the long hot day. She hangs in her work of art, the art that feeds her, her messy zippered signature saying, "I am here."

Two days ago, I drove for ten hours on I-40, one segment of my sixteen-hour journey. Most of the time I drove in absolute silence, cruise control set at 77 mph, humming along in my little cocoon of steel. However, a friend had sent me the link to a podcast hosted by Julia Louis-Dreyfus, an interview with one of my favorite authors, Isabel Allende, so somewhere west of Albuquerque, I put in my earbuds and began to listen.

Allende spoke of feminism and generations. "We were a transitional generation. . . . We were raised like our mothers, but we had to act like our daughters." When I stop for gas, I pull out my journal, write down her words, slammed by this truth, even for my generation, though Allende is a few years older than my mother.

When I near the center of Albuquerque, I long to take the exit I took three weeks ago, north to Pilar, a little riverside village south of Taos where my daughter, Lily, lives and works for a river rafting company. I loved being there with her, sleeping head to foot in the camper trailer, sitting on the smoking porch laughing and listening to music, tubing down the Rio Grande in the evening. All those free people, comfortable in their own skins, turning their backs on the nine-to-five existence to do seasonal work, living in close community. Ink and boobs and bellies and bare feet, wild hair and smoke. So far removed from my grandmother's strictures about decorum, "no white after Labor Day," hats in church, and pantyhose. And my mother's ideas of covering up my arms so I didn't look heavy and no swimsuits cut up high on the thighs. I loved seeing those women in bikinis and those barefoot men with painted toenails. I decided to love my own poochy belly.

But on this day, I must continue driving east to see my own mother. She has Alzheimer's disease and my father, her caregiver, is getting tired. I am going to give him some relief. As I continue to drive, I feel like a push-me-pull-me, stretched and pulled between my mother's generation and my daughter's. Though, when I go to look up the Dr. Dolittle reference, it is actually Pushmi-Pullyu in the book, so I've even got that wrong. Midlife is messy.

My mother colors carefully and neatly, with colored pencils, in adult coloring books. And reads labels, even my tattoos, "Hike your own hike." A peal of laughter. "Like a teenager!" she editorializes. I am glad the vintage valentine on my thigh that says "Well Fuck" is covered up. My father does all of the laundry, keeps house to a degree, though Rosa and her daughter came this morning ("Hispanic," remarks my mother as she watches them get out of the car) and had this house spotless in about three hours. Rosa hugged me when she left, murmuring in my ear, "You are so patient."

Ha. If only.

Dad keeps the bird feeders filled and the natural stone birdbath full of water since Pedro, the arthritic horse, thirty-plus years old, drinks from it as well. So we sit at the kitchen island and I keep Mom in snacks, cut-up strawberries ("Why did I wait so long to taste THESE!") and a banana, and watch the birds out the window until the red squirrel shows up with his acrobatics, worth every stolen seed for the entertainment factor.

My father tells me stories about when he and Mom courted, and I find out, after all these years, that she made the first move, a high school sophomore inviting the college man to one of her volleyball games, extending the invitation via one of his friends. He delves into politics, an anomaly in my life since I was raised, for the most part, in an apolitical household. The current climate has jumped so many out of complacency and their ability to ignore current events. "I don't like to talk about politics," he says, "because I don't want to drive a wedge between myself and those I love. I am a lifetime Republican. I'm discovering that the reason some lifelong Republicans can stomach voting for Trump is because of one issue: abortion. But if Prohibition taught us anything, it is that we can't legislate morality. If we outlaw abortion, where will women go? To a speakeasy, a back-alley doctor who will do it anyway. Just like bootleg booze. I never want anyone to kill a baby, but the law is not the way to keep that from happening. Capturing their hearts for Jesus is the way, not Trump." He also talks with me about the Harris/Walz ticket ("Finally someone who has studied civics!"), and I almost cry with relief. We have at least this common ground, and I can say "Jesus" as a euphemism for almost anything so it sounds like we are on the same page. He calls my sister an "extreme women's libber" and I laugh on the inside—if he only knew! But I am here for common ground, not debate. Is it love that makes me choose peace and harmony or simply my tendency to avoid conflict?

This is the place where I feel the double helix of DNA twisting through my veins. I am among the people who share my genetic makeup . . . skin, hair, bones, facial features, sense of humor, love for animals and the natural world, propensity for minimalism, the shared possibility of both longevity and a basketful of diseases: breast cancer, heart condition, and Alzheimer's.

One shared trait is exhibited at 5 a.m.—a love of rising early into silence and solitude, three of the four of us retreating to our own puddles of gentle light with hot beverage of choice, only murmured good mornings, all of us preferring to encounter no one for the first two hours, if possible. I don't remember a time in my life when I rose in the same house with my mother that I didn't find her having "quiet time with the Lord," as I sought out the coffee pot. Now, robbed of personality and habits and direction by dementia, she sleeps in while my brother, my father, and I pass each other in the hallway on the way to our chairs.

The gene spiral I most hope prevails is that of my grandfathers, since the men live long in this family. My father's heart attack on Christmas Day, shortly after he turned 80, was, more than likely, a result of diet since he's spent his life considering Little Debbie, Hostess, and Diet Coke to be predominant food groups. Both of my grandfathers lived into their mid-90s, and my father is likely to now that he has four stents to keep the arteries open and flowing.

In this place, among those who share my blood, I cannot escape my past full of mistakes and nervous chatter. I am branded forever as one who "talks a lot," powerless to change that label though in my real life I am silent for days at a time. I face also my possible future. I don't know if I have the genetic marker for Alzheimer's, the disease that took my mother's mother and now has taken her, though I spat in the vial for a blind study. And I indeed feel blind as I eliminate toxins from my environment and diet as much as possible, digging into the cabinet for the percolator I sent my parents years ago. I'll never take statins to lower cholesterol, and I am happy to eat healthy fats. No pesticides sprayed in my garden or house, no artificial sweeteners and very little sugar since we now know how harmful both are to the brain and Alzheimer's disease has also been labeled type-3 diabetes. My biggest indulgence is a little whiskey on ice in the evenings, and I can justify it all day long just as my father justifies pouring Diet Coke into my mother's favorite cup all day long. I don't mention microplastics or the landfill as the Keurig gurgles and hums through the morning—it is too late for that.

I worry about the garden spider should they decide to spray some hideous chemical in the yard, domesticating the wildness around them, just as I feel the chains of domestication here, a pull to be who they would have me be rather than the autonomous self I have crafted apart from them, indeed hiking my own hike, long past adolescence. My mother asks if my "butterflies hurt," meaning my collarbone tattoo. I tell her that tattoos are jewelry that lasts forever, and my previously rigid and intolerant mother says, "Oh, I like that! They are pretty!" Blessings come with the curse.

When I am with my daughter, I do not wish to fix her, change her, advise her, but rather I wish to be her—emulate her—live as a mouse in her pocket—go on the road with her, dirt-bag my way from hot springs to riversides to hunting lodges in swamps to trails through the wilderness, turn back time and choose adventure rather than prescription, freedom and choice rather than duty and obligation, seasonal work rather than a humdrum existence, year in and year out. She, too, has thrown off the ties of over-domestication.

Since I can't turn back time, I revel in the Spotify playlist we build together, training my ear to appreciate new and different sounds, new melodies, new artists. I rethink my relationship with foundational garments and the natural shape of my body, vowing to love my belly from now on. I find myself living from her example rather than that of my elders, my mother and my grandmothers who, though they could vote, were still restricted by hand-me-down rules of dress and behavior, if maybe not legislation. Though free to do so, they didn't have their own bank accounts or credit cards solely in their names. They went on very few adventures. My mother and her mother both had careers but never left the house without a bra and a full face of Mary Kay makeup until dementia took away even those habits. They never floated a river with a cold beer and a few puffs, fully relaxed. They were constantly vigilant from cradle to almost-grave. So, now I find myself asking, "What would Lily do?" as I sail east on the wave of Allende's voice. She speaks of aging and sex, creative process and discipline. She laughs with Julia about the marijuana blueberries that help her forget the current manuscript she is writing, enhance her sex life at 80, and aid her sleep.

Perhaps here in this season, raised like my mother but acting like my daughter, pulled in many directions, sleeping in Texas while my work in Arizona is being neglected, I am molting like the cardinals, my feathers bedraggled. My bright season both behind me and coming around again.

Or maybe I am a silly squirrel, hanging by my back feet to steal seed from both generations.

No, I am the garden spider, weaving a web of connection and sustenance, signing it with my own beautiful name, the double helix of who I am.

PERSONALITIES ON JANUARY 6

Thin and old, ears edged with gray—he sticks his head around the tailgate as I put coffee on the camp stove, five a.m. An old shipper bull volunteered into camp last night, singing an ancient ballad in a forgotten key. He wears a year brand; we've done the math. Bought from Webb's when he was two, so that makes him thirteen now. Whipped out by the young bucks, he's been living solitary off in some lonely canyon. Drawn now to the sound of social . . . babies bawling over the roar of branding pot, shippers protesting, perhaps even the distant memory of hay thrown out into dusty pens. He hung around overnight. Perhaps he finds me odd, this woman, frying Spam and eggs, smelling of burnt hair and horse sweat, black coffee and sleep, the blood of his great-grandsons splattered on my shirt—this woman, feral around the edges, for whom luxury is ice in her evening drink, the promise of a shower three days from now.

Whatever this old bull thinks, or what I think, life moves on from our dawn tailgate communion.

Someday I'll ride home. Someday he'll get on the truck . . . unless he disappears again, singing his rusty old song.

This life lends itself to recognition of personalities like that old bull. From the horses to the cows to the ravens who are friends

113

with the dogs, playing tag from tree to tree, from the mean rooster I threaten with the shovel to the audacious, white-socked gray cat rolling in the dirt in front of the barn. The bald eagle in the syca-more, staking out my chicken pen.

This morning, I left my desk when the dogs barked, heralding a visitor. Before the pandemic, I would have invited Jake in for coffee and the last of the gingerbread, but instead, we stood in the cold wind in front of the house. Jake is our Wildlife Manager, and he stops by from time to time, especially during hunting season, and sometimes it seems like it is always the season to kill something. Right now, he tells me, it is archery season for deer and javelina. We wrap our arms around ourselves and move further into the sunshine. No, Gail isn't here. He had a doctor's appointment in town. Jake's children are six and eight now. How is that possible? He tells me about taking them hunting on Sunday, the greatest pig hunt ever. People here call javelina "pigs" though they aren't porcine at all. They are peccaries, more akin to rodents. He tells me about taking the whole family and how they hiked up to a ridge and had a picnic and the kids got to dig holes in the dirt. How few people realize the importance of being able to dig holes when you go hunt-ing. You have to be six and eight to understand. And how he sat up there with them, glassing down below, and how a doe and her fawn tiptoed up behind them and they all got to watch the pair flee through the trees. And how he saw a herd of javelina and discussed with the kids how he would try to get close enough for a shot and how he walked down the ridge and a boar turned broadside and how he missed. And how much fun it was that they all got to go hunting and picnicking and hole digging, and how he got a decent shot but didn't end up having to touch a filthy pig.

We laughed there in that January light.

The dogs sat at my feet as the conversation moved on. They know Jake from previous visits. We spoke of government, such a compli-cated word lately. We spoke of how government and its agencies, one of which pays his living, several of which have oversight on this place that is my home, work best individual to individual, about how relationships are more important than regulations and rhetoric and people more important than politics and policies, about how cooperation is more likely to happen if we know his agency as Jake and Darren and Tom and Jesse and Matt rather than by some capital letter acronym. We stopped talking as three little does stepped like marionettes through the brown horse pasture. When we broke our silence, and Jake headed back to his office in town, I stood a moment longer realizing that he was the first person other than my husband I'd seen in three full weeks.

I retreated to the warm house and my laptop. One of the tabs was open to the *New York Times* live coverage of the certification of the 2020 presidential election. A friend who is a political historian has been explaining to me that in good times, we tend to ignore the underpinnings of government. In bad times, in times of unrest, all of a sudden we wish we'd paid more attention in civics class. I moved the mouse and clicked over.

Personalities roared across my screen. A bare-chested man in a horned hat. An anonymous mob of mostly white middle-aged men taking selfies and wearing T-shirts with heinous slogans. Violence erupting in a place where the halls are hallowed. Pundits trying to analyze with no information to analyze. Leaders leading. Leaders cowering. Leaders pandering to the personality of that mob.

Two women carrying a box between them to safety.

I wish I knew their names.

MY WITCHES

In a closet, on a shelf, in an album with black paper pages, old photographs show six women in silver bathing suits standing on a parade float holding brooms covered in glitter and wearing pointy black hats. Their hair was perfect, even under the brutal summer sun. They were hips-cocked pin-up-girl fancy, younger than I am now, the most glamorous women in West Texas. They were The Witches, my grandmother and her best friends.

In the summer of 1936, the town of Fort Stockton created a festival to commemorate the Texas Centennial while also paying tribute to the beautiful springs that contributed so much to the region. The tradition continues today. The beauty pageant and synchronized swimming are arranged around a new theme every year, a theatrical spectacle in an Olympic-sized rectangle of pale blue water in a greasewood desert. My grandmother and her friends joined in the celebration that first year dressed as witches with silver brooms. They participated every year after that according to the theme, but they were always known for their creative costumes that first summer.

When I was growing up, my family didn't celebrate Halloween and my mother greatly disapproved of anything to do with evil or magic or paganism. She always made a face of disapproval and sighs of dismissal when anyone mentioned The Witches or we turned the page of the photo album to the images of those wonderful wild women. Of course, my mother also disapproved of the fact that my grandmother and her friends drank alcohol and smoked cigarettes, at least until everyone quit smoking. The Witches met for lunch every Wednesday at K-BOB's Steakhouse, year-round, and when I stayed with my grandparents in the summer, I got to go, too, a tiny frog in their midst.

My mother had her own group of friends, organized loosely around faith and cups of coffee and nursing babies. The thing I remember most is that they showed up. They showed up for each other. They showed up with casseroles at funerals and Bible studies. They showed up with recipes and garden truck and advice. With prayers and elbow grease. They cared for one another's children and listened to one another's woes while we hopped around their feet. One of my mother's best friends was the midwife who delivered my baby brother, standing at the foot of the bed, holding her hands and bracing as my mother put her feet on her enormous, capable thighs as she pushed. Another showed up to sit in waiting with my father during the hours before birth. For years, until dementia robbed her of her daily routines, my mother called that friend every morning for Bible reading and prayer.

We all have something in our past that keeps us small and safe. We name those reins and hobbles anew as we grope for comforting confines in our present. Again and again they draw us into the boxes where we function best. Or sleep.

I am an eldest child—for years, the responsible one. Even as I imagine I have left that role behind, I make lists and by god get the job done. My husband says I *scurry*. Likewise, my father used to say that my mother's tennis shoes were smoking. Perhaps, like me, she was terrified of letting someone down.

For so long, I smiled and tried not to make waves. I was accommodating. I am less so now in the middle of my sixth decade. And yet, I continue to work each day not to be a bother, not to become someone's duty and obligation. Who wants to be a fire that someone else must tend . . . or put out?

In my mid-30s, I thought I fell in love with another woman, a woman I see now was but a clear mirror of my own inner passion and drive and ambition and desire to leave a narrow life, seeking something bigger, something more, a broader definition. But I sometimes grieve the actual flesh-and-blood woman I fell for back then. She popped out in my writing as metaphor. A man I was in relationship with later read the manuscript and said, "People will think you are a lesbian. And you spelled Ziploc wrong." I still spell ziplock about four different ways and left the smallness of that man, too. He listened to Rush Limbaugh on his car radio and said things like, "If we were together for real, you'd have to take that thing out of your nose." I had recently gotten a tiny cubic zirconia bling to sparkle on my face. I was in the process of finding out my own proclivities, not for other women, but for men who kept me small. But safe.

Though that woman is gone from my life now, I follow her rising star on social media and remember a long-ago night when she and I sat together on a red velvet sofa in a crowded tapas bar. I longed to break the bonds of "nice Texas girl from a good background," and had just figured out what *tapas* means.

"I added to it, see?" A phoenix rising from the ashes of her past is tattooed on the small of her back. That evening, in a conservative West Texas music town, she lifted the hem of her denim sundress. Her white cotton panties glowed brilliant against her thighs and the red sofa. I viewed the addition to the ink on her back. The desire to be brave rose in my belly and crowded the back of my throat as I touched the feathers of that myth with my index finger.

That evening she told me a story of betrayal and miscommunication and broken promises, about being presented with a contract with the potential to rob her of her creative fire and ability to captain her own ship.

I kicked off my own shoes beneath the sofa, sipped my own wine as my knees touched hers, our feet tangled between us. The bars of my personal cage didn't break so much as fade and melt when she shrugged off the untenable contract. "I wiped my pussy with it."

I came late to the concept of friendship with women, but that encounter, that courage, that spitting in the face of established norms, set the bar high for the kind of women I wanted to inhabit the sacred spaces in my life.

Most of my prior friendships were superficial and sprang from physical proximity, such as living on the same ranch, or shared interests like homeschooling or children around the same age. It has only been in the last two decades that I have found my circle of badass wild women, almost entirely online, spread out over distance, the proximity of ideas and similar goals and like minds bringing us together. A love of words and books and deep diving into concepts and discussions. In our circle, we check in with one another daily, sometimes hourly, holding each other's hands across the miles.

We are disparate not only in geography but in life . . . some of us in agriculture, some city dwellers. We are artists, authors, researchers, mothers, child-free, grandmothers, aunties, musicians, students, historians, advertising executives, daughters holding the hands of aging mothers, and, in this decade, sisterfriends, as messy midlife swirls around us, meeting up via WhatsApp and email and other communication platforms rather than over weekly plates loaded at a K-BOB's salad bar.

We show up for each other. We cast our spells of secrecy around the hard parts when we vent and then must repent. We hold each other's hands and say, "Put your feet on my thighs. I will help you push that beautiful idea into the world." We shower each other with confetti when we need to celebrate the tiny daily successes like we got out of bed and we made it through. We read each other's contracts and rail against those who would rein us in. We may not always synchronize how we swim through the world, but we clink glasses of friendship potion and splash each other with ear of newt, moan about men, moan about teenagers, moan about aging parents and grown children, reach out from various caves and beckon, "Light the fire under the cauldron and help me stir troubles into bubbles and mist." We hold each other's feet to the fire and correct each other's spelling. We chant the songs of wild places and take pictures of the domestic and the birds at the seed feeders. We light candles for each other, send dirty jokes via text message, books and chocolate and birthday cards via the postal service.

We are a coven of smart wild women and we hold glittery brooms that shine through the night. Beacons to indicate where we need to show up next with big feminine energy, and maybe a casserole.

BUILDING FIRES

I 've pulled up, let everyone ride ahead of me in the trot line. I came here thinking I was tough, that I could learn to do almost anything. Three days later my heart lay defeated on cold ground, beneath a sky too big, beside rocks too hard and brush too thick and slopes too steep and shouted orders coming too fast and too complicated.

I know nothing.

Tomorrow, I'll cinch up all wrong.

After only a decade of self-doubt and uncertainty, I sit by the fire and almost know the right questions to ask, make a few cow drives almost in the right place. Block a trail without being told, almost. The shouter stops mid-shout when he sees I am already there. Throw my loop in the dirt twice in a pen of fifteen calves. Start asking a different set of questions.

But there are spurs on my feet and a sweated hat on my head and my saddle is no longer new. I should oil it on a Sunday afternoon. Five or six miles away, cobwebs sully the corners and laundry piles beside my unmade bed because this morning I crawled out from under this canvas, donned these filthy clothes, to start this dawn fire while horses chewed their way through hay and grain.

I am a key player in the day's game, flank up after we shove 'em through the gate, spend the whole morning tucking cows back in—walk along, girls, walk along.

The sky spreads from edge to edge doing a true west stretch.

In the corrals, we continue the horseback dance, sorting the herd, but I'm still smoothing out the turns and steps and bends. This mare knows the dance better than I do, all twinkle toes and grit, and I laugh when we are done. Slide off to help kindle a different fire, pull my cinch extra tight—we've got some big longears to brand in this bunch. I wish I had started learning to rope when I was eight instead of thirty-eight.

I have learned not to count the unbranded calves in each bunch. I am learning, also, to let go of the fumbling anxiety about how much work looms ahead and how inept I am at the tasks at hand. Calf by calf, we work our way through, and I'm finally at a place where I can joke with the crew, built loop resting in my right hand. One of the few times in my life when I've felt graceful, when I've found grace.

I know the drive to Mud Spring—could do it in my sleep. Or the rain. Or the almost dark. Hold 'em up on water before trotting back to camp for two "cowboy cool" beers fished from the water trough, my shirt damp with sweat, salt from my lips on the rim of the can, the sun boiling the evening clouds. Throw hay to the cattle going to the sale barn tomorrow and water the horses and look at the crack in Bonnie's hoof.

Break up some wood, tiny twigs and tree bark, blow hard—I'm building another fire. Beef from the cooler and scent of smoke while patties sizzle—no more hair on my knuckles, the chuckles of cooking over wood. Camp buttoned up for the night and our bed rolled out on the ground, I stand in the early dark, not ready to lie down.

The sky is still too big, the rocks are still too hard, the brush is still too thick, the slopes still rise above, neverending. None of that has changed. But there is a fire overhead that I didn't build and I'm carrying one of my own.

It burns hot behind my eyes.

COYOTE BITCH

When a horse has a lot of endurance, a lot of heart, gives all it has to the job or miles at hand, we say they have a lot of "bottom."

Because I am only four foot ten and one-half inches tall, weighing in at about 110 pounds, I will never be physically powerful. I learned early on that if I am to do this job, I have to outthink, rather than outmuscle, many tasks—learn to use leverage and timing more than brute strength.

But, when I swing up into the saddle, the horse between my knees is an equalizer. I can go as far, do as much, as anyone, and when we are working cows, I have the advantage of actually having experienced ovulation, gestation, and lactation like the animals we care for. I have given birth. And, it is possible that I might try harder than the extra men we hire because I care more about getting the job done, and done well. When the day is over, they draw their pay and go home. I live here.

Right now, all the horses in my string are mares. They love to work cows. They have a lot of bottom.

◈

He said I was bossy, threw the word at me from the time I was very small. Threw it like a dart I was too young to dodge, not like a softly lobbed ball for me to catch and make my own. That dart made a wound in my chest, stuck there firmly for years. I am the oldest of his four children; he is the youngest of five. He had two bossy older sisters. Now, forty years removed, I can see that his labeling me bossy long before I could ever *be* bossy was more about him than it was about me. His story is long and complicated. My part of the story is age-old: a small girl told not to be bossy and that *big sisters are the crabgrass in the lawn of life*. He got the phrase from a *Peanuts* cartoon long before I understood what crabgrass was. Long before I had a lawn. But I understood, even then, by context and tone, that crabgrass was something undesirable, something bad, something wrong. Something to be eliminated.

The man in our living room, having a drink beside our fire, is an investment expert. He will help you with your money if you will pay him to do so. He has just reviewed my fourth book in his online newsletter, but truly, he would rather talk about his own book, a how-to book, soon to be released, self-published. He will tell us all about how to do it.

He asks me if I have considered getting serious about my writing.

I can feel my husband on high alert beside me, silently begging me to "be nice," while I sit in shock thinking, "Fuck nice."

Finally, I realize he doesn't mean writing . . . he means marketing. He knows methods and prescriptions and numbers—I am sure he could teach Hemingway a thing or two, but he'd run if he ever caught a glimpse of the White Goddess. She's a scary bitch.

Still, I'd hire him to do my marketing. He can walk the streets from bookstore to gift shop carrying stacks of books only to have teenage clerks tell him to come back on Tuesday when the purchasing manager will be in. He revises. What he really means is that I should write something of regional interest.

I look at him for a long pause in the flow of words. Regional. I see. So, I should aim smaller, not bigger.

I take a sip of my whiskey as the faltering conversation moves on, no segue, no help from me because I am being nice. I am so glad this man explained things to me. No way would I allow him to invest my money, regionally.

He said, "I don't know how good of a hand she is, but she makes a great cow dog!" This after I slid off, threw him my bridle reins, and dug those two heifers out of the boulder pile where a horse can't go because I care more about not leaving anything behind than I do about some cowboy image. I know he disapproves of a woman in cow camp, even if she does bring in her share of cows and does all of the cooking.

In a fight with my husband, he says, "Don't be shrill." Later in the day, I play a song by P!NK. Turn up the volume.

I sat in the greenroom of a cowboy poetry gathering and listened while a white, middle-aged man told me how uncomfortable one of my books made him because I wrote about all of that *woman stuff*, the biology of being female. He thinks I shouldn't mention the uncomfortable details of it all. From where I sat, I could see his wife across the room. He has four daughters. He owns cows.

He said, "We all have something." Driving along a rural high-way and he is playing "educate Amy," which includes lessons in philosophy, music, art, and methodology delivered with a developing jargon he is practicing on me, open to discussion.

I follow along behind his thoughts and pick up crumbs and pearls of wisdom. Some of his words I have dropped back onto the path, like flint chippings tossed aside. That shining shard may have been flaked off the bigger chunk of obsidian while forming a point, but I am after the real deal, fully formed and useful.

But I've kept that phrase. *Everyone has something.*

He meant it as an argument to leave our excuses behind. He meant, "Get over it." Each of us has something that keeps us small, something that holds us back, something that silences true voice. Everyone has a wound. But as we carry a stone along on our way, we rub and wear it, polish the lessons and the gift. Turn it over with the pads of our fingers until we know the edges and indentations intimately. This intimacy allows the wisdom to emerge. The beauty shines through when we stop seeing it as it applies only to self, listing *my* somethings, a long line of somethings that need to be laid aside so that I might walk on. When I begin to see that others have something, the seeds of empathy swell and burst and sprout. The spiral dance continues, and we come back around, always, only we are never the same. I begin to see my own somethings as less than wounds or weights and more as elements of individuality and voice, my own shining jewels in a unique setting. And I begin to look for the gifts another brings to the chorus.

Everyone knows what I *should* be writing during my publishing drought. My friends and I call this *should-ing* all over someone. *Dig deep, don't be shallow, but make sure there is an uplift. Cut to the bone, into the heart of the matter, but be kind. No need for an exposé. Entertain me, but we live in crazy times and you can't ignore the strife or insulate yourself here in this big place. That would be elitist. Make*

me cry but give me hope. Sometimes your writing is too long; sometimes your writing is too sparse. What you should really write is a movie script or a book that can be turned into a movie. That is where the money is. You are in a unique place, but make it matter to the average Joe on the street. Why don't you write a sequel to that story about Uncle Bill? Write something marketable, something that everyone in the room can get excited about. Be careful not to cross the line between prose and poetry and I can't find the line.

I drink from a cup of wolf energy today and fall in love with the word keen. Both a note of lament that cuts through the wind and a sharp edge, keen is a two-bitted word, a tool-and-voice word. It is two hours before dawn.

To yearn for world peace is to ask the slinking coyote not to feed her den of mewling pups a cute bunny rabbit, loose fur blowing away in the wind; to ask the eagle and hawk to draw in their talons; to ask the bear to leave the grubs below ground and dine only on berries; to ask the mountain lion not to break the neck of the fleeing fawn. Peace does not come from a life without strife, a life without tearing into the meat of things.

Peace is not a global condition, and it never will be. Peace springs first from naming and recognition and telling the truth even when it is uncomfortable. Peace is a choice, achieved inwardly, unseen, a state we fight for. We do battle with our own inner voices until we manage to get them all lined up in a harmonious chorus that lasts one song, one early dawn, one pass along the scale—and we turn to our slate and write, *I am at peace.* Before the chalk is finished scratching, the chorus breaks and begins squabbling again. But we hear echoes of the song and remember it on into our lives until it becomes habit to call on the inward peace, spreading like a stain if we allow it.

The coyote bitch, licking her favorite daughter's fragile ears after the feast, does not know her own reputation.

LOVEGOD

It is fall. The juniper berries have turned loose to become blue puddles beneath the trees, hard to explain to someone who has never seen how vibrant colors are here in the desert. This is not a popular tourist area. The sightseers are looking up at the foliage in the standard houses of autumn worship, but I have blue puddles beneath the trees.

And wasp galls. To be specific, apple wasp galls. A wasp called the oak apple gall wasp, *Amphibolips confluenta*, causes apple galls on the oak trees. Or rather, the oak tree reacts to a part of the wasp's life cycle by creating an "apple" around its larval stage.

The oak trees are loaded with apples this year.

I walk beneath the apples and atop the blue puddles with two dogs weaving a net of connection around me. They always come bounding back. And I think about the evolution of something as amazing as a juniper tree or a blackjack oak or a wasp or a puppy. And the evolution of my own faith. I have embraced the words from my youth about working out our own salvation with fear and trembling. Only, I don't . . . or won't . . . or can't . . . believe that babies are born sinful and in need of saving. Babies are born as whole worlds unto themselves in need of nurture and care that allow them to become who they are meant to become. We create bubbles of love around our babies. Like apples around a wasp embryo.

And while I still tremble in awe, I have let the fear go. I post photographs of rattlesnakes and spiders on my social media and people react with horror, a horror I cannot comprehend. A rattle-snake or a spider is not evil.

The whole world is a mirror.

Like water, we choose the path of least resistance, but then, it behooves us, like the mountain goat, to climb to the tallest point for a different view. I am, as the Apostle Paul said, the least of these. I cannot consider something as unknowable as the wasp gall—a wound by one creature causing another creature to form a womb for the larvae of the first—and imagine that I am better than or more than those creatures. It does not humble me to consider that Christ died for my sins in the middle of this contemplation. On a personal level it seems ludicrous. On a cultural level it seems more noise to keep me from sitting still in the dirt like a dung beetle . . . considering the apple gall and the life it contains.

Does the sting of the wasp contain the coding to tell the oak leaf how to form a proper place of incubation? May I break one open to see the fine filaments holding the developing embryo dead center of the apple, and thus, in my curiosity, kill it? Do I call it science or research or abortion? Hard questions to contemplate from down here in the dirt; the ethics, the morals, the biology, the beauty.

Please save me from this miracle.

A friend teaches Songwriting 101 at a university and laughs each fall when he begins scheduling individual meetings with his students. When he asks what their song is about, they invariably say, "Loooooove," and he gets them on track with questions like what kind of love and how is this different from every damned songwriting 101 student before them.

One recent evening I was in my office when my husband came through the door saying, "I brought you a sad present." In his hands he held a kestrel–dead, of course, which is what makes it sad. The wild thing broke its neck hitting our huge picture windows, those panes of glass that keep out the wild things.

What makes it love is that he knew I would be thrilled to hold this creature in my hands, examining the feathers as soft as visible nothing, moving the talons, lifting the eyelids to see the black, feeling the hook of its perfect meat-eating beak, cradling it in my arms as we stood outside in the setting sun. I longed to preserve this dead body without inevitable odor and maggots. It was still warm, had breathed moments ago.

Gail stood there watching me with the dead bird, never saying "gross," not wanting more gift than this one, right now, and I know that when they hand out awards for loving, he'll get his.

We are looking for love. The fallacious hope that persists in flavoring our pursuit is that love will be perfect. We have a vision of perfection, even those of us who have, in the past, had a perfect love that revealed itself to be flawed and faded. For surely, the loves of our past were flawed because of who, not what. Surely the fault was in the person, not in the concept, the big idea. For after all, isn't god the definition and embodiment of love?

Each day dawns to be perfect and is then marred by our expectations, by what we view in the news, or how long our list of errands is, or how fat we feel, or who shit on our mood. Is the fault with the news, the chores, body image, or him, or her? Or is the fault in our viewing and today was wonderful and perfect and right after all? Today is just as it should be.

We reach for god, the perfect ruler and holder of life, an idea bigger than any one or one thousand or one million of us. Perhaps we've had a glimpse of the essential concept. We've stood on the perfect beach in the perfect sunset with the perfect dress flowing in the perfect breeze. The perfectly handsome man went down on one knee and offered the perfect ring and the perfect life. If that is our vision of god and love, we have a long way yet to go. In a few years, the bathroom stinks in the morning as that perfectly handsome man rushes out the door for work, banging the door we've asked him not to bang.

Perhaps we had a glimpse of the essential concept when we held a newborn in our arms and felt a moment of unflawed and pure and intense joy as we saw ourselves mirrored in new life. This is what we've been seeking—this, finally, is true love. But then the earth resumes turning, and we bleed onto the sheets and the diaper fills with yellow cottage cheese, and our nipples crack and bleed and this new piece of life—of us—screams for four hours straight. Is it love or hormones? We pull up the photo of the moment when it was perfect, hoping to remember, and there we are, puffy-faced from pushing with sweaty stringy hair, medical equipment all around for what was supposed to be an all-natural birth in a room we toured months ago with beautiful décor and muted colors on the walls. And we see, in the photo, not a picture of perfection in our arms but a pufferfish. A red writhing pufferfish indistinguishable from every other new human in the minutes after being pushed rudely into the light. It was true love, and the cranky toddler at our feet is not the one who is flawed.

Love is the dog that can't make up his mind to come in or out. Love is the husband who says biting words after his second drink at night and wipes his hands on his jeans when he eats bacon in the morning. Love is a child who grows up, decides I'm toxic, and, for a period of time, removes their love. Yes, that, even that, is love. Even that is god. It is when we give god a gender, a capital letter, a voice, a human-style benevolence and a golden halo, that we fail to see what love looks like, we fail to see god in our lives.

There is no such thing as unconditional love. We always love with condition. With the condition that that which we love is that which we love, even if it shifts and changes. But not too much. And we are loved on the condition that we are who we are.

Love is cold wind, too many events on the calendar, guests arriving, and we don't have enough towels. It is telling someone to go to hell and meaning it. It is a leader who grabs pussies, justice and injustice, drama and peace, drought and flood, a human struggling to find his voice and missing the mark. Love is watching someone waste time and life. Love is wasting our own time and our own lives as we are the nematode hatching, waiting to be reborn as glorious. We are forgotten gardens, moldy cheese in the refrigerator, tasks that we don't want to do because surely, if we had enough money, enough education, enough skill, enough time, enough luck, enough, well, love . . . it would all be better, and we could sit back and enjoy the day.

Or what if what we have right now is love. Is god. What if lovegod is all of it.

And it is good . . .

THE PINCH HITTER

"**G**ood morning to one of my favorite people!" Randy gets in the passenger seat after I pull up to the bunkhouse. It is one of the nicest greetings from someone I have folded into my family of choice. "Who won the game last night?" He is teasing me gently and I know he doesn't really care what my answer is. Like a lot of people, Randy finds it odd that I am a baseball fan, though a fan only in postseason play. I try to explain: a chess game with statistics and physics that can turn in a heartbeat played by athletic skilled smart men in tight pants . . . what's not to love?

Today is a "town day." We live forty-five minutes from the nearest gallon of gas or gallon of milk, so we both have lists. Lists upon lists. The first few miles are spent discussing where all we need to stop, our personal items impossible to tease apart from ranch stuff since True Value Hardware has chainsaw oil, plumbing parts, and the best gift selection in town. One of my dearest girlfriends has a birthday soon. My eye is on my lists and the road. Randy is studying his little notebook. We line out our day.

When we still have about fifteen miles to go, Randy shifts into "things I have been thinking about" mode. The three of us, Randy, Gail, and I, all live at Spider Ranch headquarters, but to get all of the jobs done, we often go our separate ways on a daily basis. It is solitary work, and Randy lives alone. "The elk drifted by this morning. You know, during my commute." Another little joke is that Randy's morning commute is coffee on the front porch of the bunkhouse. "I've worked all of my life, almost every day of my life, and I wake up some mornings now and want to shout for joy that I live and work on the Spider."

Randy is good at jerking my own errant thinking back into perspective, especially on days when I want to run away to Hawaii, though I've had enough birthdays to realize that Hawaii or Boston or Paris won't fix any niggling discontent in the long term because where I go, there I am.

"I've always, before, had at least an hour commute, going to work and coming home a big expense. You know, gas money."

Several times since coming to live in the bunkhouse as the ranch handyman, caretaker, and occasional cowboy—our pinch hitter—the one who can fix dang near anything, use any tool, drive heavy equipment, the one who adds value to everything he touches, whether it is garden soil or the tractor or the branding pen, Randy has tried to shove money in my hand for gas since I carry him to town for appointments or, like today, when his list includes the bank, smoke shop, and grocery store scattered amongst our other stops. "Oh, I need a new pair of gloves." His musings are interrupted as he pulls out his little notebook again.

"Today just elk traffic. I didn't see those javelina or the coyotes." He fingers his phone, a reluctant addition to his life that I insist on and maintain for him so we can text back and forth while I am on remote parts of the ranch and he is left with the full responsibility of headquarters, my dogs, and extra horses.

"Did we get paid?" I answer yes. Twice a month. Always. Every two weeks. "So, I'll need to check." One of Randy's biggest worries is banking via phone app and the direct deposit method that the payroll company uses. He hates not having paper statements. Silently, I vow to print out the last few months for him after we get home.

"It's hard, you know. I am not sure I am doing enough. I mean, no one checks on my work or tells me what to do. . . . Sometimes it feels like I get paid just to live here."

Randy hasn't stopped working since he arrived at the ranch. Every blade I own, from chainsaw to camp ax to kitchen knives, is sharper than brand new. If he sees a problem, like the squatty oak tree in our way when sorting cattle, a problem I have dealt with for years, he fixes it. "Should I limb it or cut it down?" He and I spent a whole afternoon trimming brush out of a corner where the smart old cows like to lie down and hide. Big things and little things, from fixing the old tractor to setting mousetraps to organizing the shop, Randy is doing everything he can to make life better. We often ended up branding on Sundays this summer because the cow sales are on Tuesdays, always aiming to haul shippers on Mondays; it just worked out this way. We told him to take Sundays off—and then promptly pulled him off the bench to help flank calves the next Sunday that came around. It is our little joke now—his days off. Gail told him last week, "Tomorrow is Sunday. Take the day off." Randy replied, "So do whatever I want?"

Randy bladed the roads at headquarters that Sunday. Doing what he wanted to do.

Today I try to set his mind at ease. "You are doing more than enough. And one reason we like having you around is that we don't have to tell you what to do. You see. You know. And I agree, living on the job is a mixed bag. Housing, utilities, beef, and no expensive commute are all great. But when to stand down . . . it becomes a personal judgement call, a matter of ethics."

I think of my own banking app. While Randy's paycheck comes in, the same amount every two weeks, mine is a different story. I am "day help." The owner asks via text for my "days" and I turn in my count. Some pay periods, my count is zero, depending on our cattle rotation schedule. Some periods it is a big number. But like Randy, I find it hard sometimes to tease apart the personal from the work since very often, those of us who work in agriculture don't have clear markers, like a commute, to separate life and work. Work is a lifestyle—and a good way to be in the world. Living is work and work is a way to live a rich full life. Turning in my days becomes a question of ethics when I am not horseback. While I may have done a dozen small ranch chores during my day, I may also have spent some hours in my office, managing online workshops and writing. I may have gone on a hike with the dogs, for fun, and checked a water gap along the way. And so, I weigh each task—until I can say, yes, I did enough to turn in a day for pay.

I admire and respect people who are passionate about their work and don't know how to leave it "at the office," or "in the studio," or "on the field." I love asking people about their lifework and listening to them talk about what they love, but I also recognize both a freedom and a bondage to living on the job.

It is a beer on the bunkhouse porch at 10 a.m. on a Sunday in July when we started branding at 6 a.m. in order to beat the heat that could kill those big bull calves we cut.

It is tying in stays all morning in October, pulling up in the afternoon to catch an East Coast playoff game that comes on at 2:08 p.m. Arizona time.

Or a day, like today—driving our pinch hitter to town for his groceries and parts for the ranch, but tailoring in a private stop for sushi and sake and reading a book or scribbling these thoughts in a notebook because the ideas are coming in fast an' hot, a curveball solidly in the strike zone. My life is a big soup of metaphor, living, work, passion—cowboying, ranch chores, writing, helping others get the words on the page, listening as my friend sorts through thoughts about how to manage a new way of being in the world.

I keep one eye on the clock.

The World Series starts tonight. East Coast Time.

O YOU SILLY WOMAN

*P*hilosophies, from Stoicism to existentialism to Salvationism to nihilism to Buddhism, have now been reduced to memes on social media. The cultish language people followed blindly to death in mass extremist movements is now used to sell skin care products, exercise regimens, and keto gummies (become a member of our team!). The psychobabble labels are like sticky notes: introvert, toxic, gaslighting, triggered, minimalism, red flags.

Let's unpack this.

Impossible to pick a metaphor and stick with it. Before my grandfather died after ninety-five years of living quite grandly and imperfectly on this planet, he made what sounded, at the time, like a silly observation, but that now strikes me as quite profound.

"All these cell phones." He waved his antiquated flip phone at us. "All these conversations flying through the air!"

A conversation carried via cables and wires was much easier for him to understand, this man who lived in a time when stringing cables and wires, laying tracks, paving highways, flying planes, and building pipelines was salvation and progress.

"Flying through the air! What happens when all those conversations start running into each other!"

We laughed.

It doesn't seem so funny now. The air is full of information and noise. Our society hangs labels above our heads as if we are pinned butterflies—main designations with subcategories below. Gender, relationships, professions, skin pigment, gold stars won or lost or misplaced, location, gods worshiped, classes taken or born into, languages spoken or forgotten. Our conversations are running into each other. We lift our voices to add our own yawp, hoping someone hears and adds the definition we most cherish. Hashtag *see me*.

My grandfather wasn't that far off in his observations. So how do we pick a metaphor? Thoreau said he went to the woods to live deliberately. Recently I walked all the way around Walden Pond, saw the site of Thoreau's cabin, drove past the Thoreau family home where his mother lived (and did his laundry and cooked lunch for him every day). We've picked holes in some of Henry David's philosophy from our lofty distance of years. I cherry-pick "deliberately" from the words he piled up. I reach over into the Stoic and existential memes for the island metaphor because it suits my lone wolf tendencies—already seeing the murky idea soup I've got cooking. As always I draw on the book I'm currently reading, thinking of the scene in *Anna Karenina* when Levin's brother dies, and from what I know of Tolstoy, it's none too difficult to see the self-portrait in Levin's fear of death, as well as his apparent awe of feminine strength and capability.

But to bring all of the threads together is impossible because try as we might, they tangle. They bump into each other in the air of our untangling.

And so, like Thoreau, I go. I go to the woods, to the flowing creek rather than the stagnant pond, to a place of privilege sans signal. Fourteen hours ago, I dropped a thirty-eight-pound pack on this creekbank, my shirt soaking wet, and my lips tasting of salt. But I was in the shade and the water is still flowing, even in June, our dry month in these mountains. I am on a mission to see a rough stretch of barbed wire fence this morning before joining the men on a corral repair project several miles from headquarters. This assignment suits me because I like bringing the dogs along, on foot, instead of using a motor. When we arrived yesterday, in the afternoon, Jim stretched full length in the shade while Bella chased water bugs and I sussed out the perfect spot for our overnight camp. After I settled in to this space where the trees block the heat, I sat in the dirt of this creekbank and put my aching feet in the water. I made a small stone hearth, gathered some light sticks and wood for my fire. I arranged the belongings I carried with me, just so, the smallest little nest in this vast place. At dusk I cooked my simple meal, fed the dogs, wrote in my journal, read my book, made recordings of the birds: warblers, vireos, woodpeckers, flickers, robins, pee-wees, towhees, quail. I reveled in relative silence, solitude, and stillness. I slept well. Now, before dawn, the chorus picks up again, here in this space, as I lean over to rekindle the fire so I might have a cup of coffee.

As the planet turns without my effort, as the smoke curls upward and the dogs disappear up canyon to check out an early morning drinker, one I will never see, I pull out my journal and prop up in my bag, waiting for hot water in my small pot.

Here is my true space. Here my presence and voice are not at all necessary, either as witness or aide or component or member of community. I arrived unheralded and unremarked and will be gone in a matter of hours, only charcoal on damp earth left behind. I am something to be avoided here, sidestepped by all the wild things who live and matter here. To them, I smell bad.

Here, miles and miles from any human habitation, is where I find it most humbling, and most appealing, to take up space. Here I recognize my own silliness in my everyday insistence on being seen and heard. Here the level of evolution both personal and universal is highlighted. Oh, you silly woman. Must you have your own room when you might have this cathedral on any evening by putting in a hard day, walking? Must you have your say when you might sit in a blessed and profound silence as the dawn wakes the world around you? Must you always insist on so much when the only one to bring you meaning and happiness is you?

O you silly woman.

Who knew, a few simple years ago, that a deficit of connectivity would become a thing of luxury? Just as the indigent in our nation have become obese, have become hoarders, so when we off-load the weight of poor nutrition and cheap goods and the constant noise of information and conversation, when we free our minds of nonstop bombardment, we are free. And so, I come to this place of luxury. To sleep in the dirt.

I sit still, my bare feet in the water. Tiny fish come to nibble a welcome.

A seep monkeyflower nods.

The vireo trills.

The sun traces a slow path through the treetops.

A lizard does push-ups on a fallen log.

The water skaters skate on the meniscus.

The air is free of clutter.

And I am here, deliberately.

Inconsequential. O you silly woman.

UNDER THE CITGO SIGN

For Cari

No matter how much time or money we spend on the formula, life rarely mirrors the pictures in magazines and the arm of the couch bears a coffee stain.

Our expectations cause us more pain and confusion than any other element in this crazy quilt of life. This is how childhood should look. See the painting? The carousel and the girl with the yellow balloon? Why didn't I get that when I was a child? Love. See the first glance, the first dance, the ring in a velvet-lined box, the white-veiled bride, the forever adoration? That is love and mine was messier and I cried more tears and it ended, and began again, and hurt. Love did not meet my expectations. Perhaps Joni Mitchell was right, and we've never known clouds or life or love at all.

Life is so very messy. It has bumps and lumps and drips. It springs leaks and takes wrong turns. Life gets lost or besieged or derailed. It scares or scars or thrills or is unutterably boring or so dramatic that the teachers tell us to sit down and be quiet. Life has peak moments and deep dark valleys, youth and age and picnics beside beautiful waters and long bedside vigils and bad cups of coffee in waiting rooms. Life is so messy that we often kick against the mess and use our energy to line all our toy soldiers up in neat rows only for the earth to shake and the wind to blow and nothing looks the way we imagined.

Recently I flew from Arizona to Boston. I left days and days of ranch work, mundane and hard, for a slice of time away. I carried with me expectations. I packed too many books and had no idea where I was headed. I was flying blind, in a way, but with a firm dialogue in my head. I would tell my dear friend, in whose apartment I had been invited to stay, to go on about her life, please don't feel obligated to entertain me. I would read my books and take walks if she'd point me down safe city streets.

I went armed and masked and ignorant, literally and figuratively. My first flight since the pandemic—no alcohol on a five-and-a-half-hour flight. But one of the best surprises in life is when all expectations get flung out the window and we fill in the gaps in our ignorance and we step outside our closed little spaces and rip down the masks and breathe deep the fresh air of something new. Dropping our expectations opens us up.

In the case of this trip to Boston, my sisterfriend laughed in the face of my ego—all self-deprecating and humble—*go on about your life while I read over here in the corner.* She took me to her nest under the Citgo sign along the bank of the Charles River. She served me intellectual conversation with helpful vocabulary to express some of the moments in this story in time. I didn't realize I was starving. She took me on a historian's tour of old Boston that included clams and calamari, death's heads, the Long Wharf, and the golden grasshopper on top of Faneuil Hall. Later in the visit she fed me lobster and Atlantic oysters and art, sea air and lighthouses and deep green woods along a muddy trail lined with brilliant fungi, conversation about privilege and how she and I, two small-town Texas girls, got from there to here. We walked along the river and up cobbled streets with gas lamps and I realized how hungry I was for ideas and exploration. We spoke of equity and equality, of the differences in medicine and the wellness industry, of photography and books and etymology. We drove past the homes of the railroad barons of the past while discussing disparity and privilege in our time. We stood together with our feet in the surf at sunset, enormous ice cream cones in our hands.

And then I flew home.

And then I saddled up to ride back into cow camp. As I unpacked more than my literal bags, I realized that our expectations can starve us, can keep us from reaching for the nutrition our souls need most, the gifts and care offered by others, and we must accept graciously in order to be graceful. Our expectations can keep us small and safe in a world that needs us open-hearted and willing to learn new things, willing to be cared for and shown a new world, a life apart from our own corner.

PREJUDICE, MINE AND YOURS

I hung a jury once. The story is one of a young ranch wife, living way out at the end of a dirt road, and a summertime small Texas town with ancient trees on the courthouse lawn, old wooden fold-down chairs in the courtroom. In obedience to the jury summons in my mailbox, I left my children with a friend, secretly excited when I was chosen to sit on the jury, a break from the monotony of my daily life, a chance for a glimpse of something besides the march of seasons, everyday meal preparation and child rearing, laundry and ranch chores. I packed a lunch to eat under those wind-sculpted trees, sitting on the old stone steps.

The judge who instructed the jury and admonished us that the burden of proof rested with the prosecution had no idea that I was one who had always taken male authority very seriously. I came from a family and a culture where those with voice were male, standing in pulpits and in roles of leadership. That judge told me that the prosecution must prove that a crime had been committed, and they didn't do it. The county attorney offered no proof other than the accusation. The other jurors had already decided, before the trial even began, that the stranger to the community, some woman's new boyfriend, not one of us, had indeed touched the woman's teenage daughter inappropriately. The trial was *he said, she said*, and I was the only one who brushed aside the *probability* that a crime had occurred and looked for the *proof* that I was told to expect.

For two long, very long, days I held out as the sole not guilty vote.

Several days later, that judge committed his own small crime by having his secretary call and invite me to chambers. From his position behind the desk, that place of authority, he said that we couldn't talk about the trial just past. His questions were more personal. Who was this person, this short woman who took his instructions seriously and caused all of this trouble?

I didn't have answers for him other than to say that I did what I was told to do, looking at the proof presented rather than prejudging.

One day last summer, I rested beside a boulder. I was weary. Two more hours, at least, to go, upcanyon, before I could lean my pack and my back on a fallen log, on a sandy bank where I have slept before, the water running shallow over slick rock with basins and pools where the hummingbirds and canyon wrens and tadpoles are abundant and busy. The elk and bear and porcupine and skunks and myriad creatures also drink in that place. I had been sent on this loop to scout for cow sign, so we would know if it was worth our while and equine muscle to ride off down in here after we move into the cabin up high on the rim in a few days. As I paused there beside the boulder, the dogs resting bellies in a pool of water in this canyon bottom, I heard *tch, tch, tch*. I stood very still, waiting until I could locate the sound. A gorgeous yellow-patterned rattlesnake lay at my feet, coiled in the shadow of the rock, politely asking me not to step on him, alerting me gently, even musically, to his presence, more polite than hostile.

Predators, those natural inhabitants of my wildish landscape, prevent me from raising a pair of peafowl or having a beehive. The bears, owls, foxes, coyotes, hawks, and eagles are as precious to me, to the grand parade, as iridescent feathers topped with a sacred eye, as the sound of a cat on two fowl feet. My natural aversion to cages and the confinement of over-domestication causes me to shy away from the chain link protection of a traditional barnyard. I don't want peacocks in a cage but strutting proudly around under an open sky full of danger. We allow our sacred beauty with its fragility to be vulnerable to the harsh predators of wild reality. The sacred and the holy are just as susceptible to the life/death/life cycle as the molecules of protein we ask to carry our symbols. The judgement belongs solely to us—the deeming of one collection of cells as higher or more holy or more sacred than another.

We humans, with our enormous capacity for imagination, have imbued certain creatures with characteristics in line with our own concepts. Some things need killing. Some things need saving. Some things are cute and clean. Others are ugly and dirty. All fires need putting out eventually. Horses are more romantic than cows. We want to return to earth as the eagle or the lion or the majestic elk, never the earthworm or the minnow or the skunk or the porcupine. Never the dung beetle, that beneficial overlooked janitor.

Is speciesism akin to racism?

Sometimes people squat on the national forest where these cows graze. It is legal to boondock for a certain period of time on public land, but most that we encounter are way past that limit. When I travel and I see community after community of cookie-cutter houses springing up on the fringes of cities, cheek to jowl with each other, I consider that even though I have never owned a home, I would prefer a tent set up in Cottonwood Canyon to one of those *little boxes made of ticky tacky . . . little boxes all the same.* I get it. I get why someone would come out here to live, and so I approach these squatters with a level of understanding. I consider that human violence derives from fear and fear is born of prejudice. Snakes are bad; kill them. The unhoused or unwashed or unfed must be weird. Avoid them.

Prejudice, mine and yours. What have we already prejudged?

What have we already made our minds up about? We eliminate whole groups of people as possible friends, allies, family . . . simply on the basis of skin color or location or language or faith or sexual orientation. We set up hierarchies of preferences, hierarchies of judgement. We have judged without hearing the evidence. We fear people who don't look like us or act like us. Some might consider it abnormal, outside of normal, not to live in a house, to live instead out in the woods, as our predecessors to this culture must have. Our cities are built where there were once woods or plains or mountains or beach.

To be called weird or weirdo is one of my grandson's biggest fears. Elementary school is full of domestication. He tells me with trembling lip that someone called him weird, and I told him, "That's okay. I am pretty weird myself." He reacted with horror. "Mamie! No, you are not!" So, I help him find a definition of weird. "Do we want everyone to be just like us? That would be boring! It is pretty cool that we are all different." He is still pondering.

The burden of proof rests with each of us. And the jury is hung.

CRUSHED, AGAIN

Dedicated, with gratitude, to Dr. Burt Faibisoff

My voice feels tiny and I'm sure so does yours
But put us all together we make a mighty roar.
　　　　　　　　—Rising Appalachia, "Resilient"

I am crushed.

"When you're lying on the floor, you can't fall out of bed."

That is how I feel this morning. It is November. October passed dry and hot with the Dodgers winning the World Series in five games, beating the Yankees, as we all endured the constant bombardment of our eardrums, brains, hearts, and souls with lies, half-truths, propaganda, racism, and horror anytime we viewed a screen. The sky refused any rain. My grandson asked me casually, as casually as if we were discussing baseball, who I thought would win the war between the Palestinians and the Israelis. To him, the volume and weight of sports, politics, and war all sound the same. He has been living with his other grandparents for a season, and he knows that Mamie won't argue politics with him, no matter what he hears in their home and parrots back at me. But he also knows that I will get into a teasing verbal tussle with him about cheering for some other team while he is absolutely devoted to his beloved Dodgers. I explained that no one wins a war—but I heard the weariness in my voice, my inability with my one infinitesimal yawp to have much effect against the noise in which he, and all children, are immersed.

In July, the men decided to clean two dry tanks here on the ranch while we waited for rain. I stood down since running heavy machinery isn't in my wheelhouse—I watered my garden and ran to town for parts until I flew to California for a speaking engagement. I returned to awful news. My guy had been unloading a 55-gallon drum of diesel from the back of the truck into the bucket of the tractor. When the drum began to slip, he reached to catch it and got his hand mashed between the heavy drum and the rim of the bucket. The accident crushed two fingers on his right hand. A severe crush injury is bad for anyone, but for someone who plays guitar and has a ranch to run, it is a double whammy. Because he wrapped the blown-out, mangled fingers in electrical tape, pulled his glove back on, and went back to work, we ended up in the emergency room a few days later for a necessary round of antibiotic and an x-ray, too late for any repairs to be done. The hand is healing, slowly, and before last week, he even picked up the guitar a few times and could, once again, rope in the branding pen.

But then, it happened again.

Sometimes I have to remind even myself that I am not making this shit up.

Another crushing injury, this time to his left hand. He was sliding a steel pipe behind some cows in the chute when the last cow backed up hard, crushing his hand between her bony hip and the pipe. Part of the ring finger is just . . . gone.

"Someone doesn't want me to play guitar," Gail joked to the emergency room doctor, who pushed his stool back from viewing the wound and said, "I can tell you right now we need to call in someone who knows reconstruction better than I do." The surgeon who came from upstairs set up a makeshift OR in the ER because it was hours before an operating room became available. He explained that he gained much of his reconstructive experience as a trauma surgeon in the Navy, operating out of a suitcase in Iraq, the Congo, and Afghanistan, the bad part. One guitar-playing cowboy needing a skin graft was nothing. He and Gail bonded over cows and airplanes while he took tiny sutures under inadequate lighting with no assistant standing by.

I sit here on this November morning, with my tiny pen and my tinier yawp, and think of a conversation I had with my friend Cari after the Democratic National Convention. She had read an article in which a political commentator questioned Kamala Harris's ability to maintain her positivity and energy.

And all the women laughed . . .

Over our tiny transcontinental connection via cell phone and Wi-Fi, Cari and I laughed.

Oh, we know. We know better than every male pundit alive. Those of us wearing Converse sneakers and pink stocking hats and "No Country for Old Men" T-shirts and whatever badass something or nothing that makes us feel badass, we know. We know how the vice president maintains her smile and that energy because we've all done it. We are doing it. In such an emergent situation, we are those who grab the keys and the wallet, the paperwork and the phone charger. We are those applying direct pressure to the wound and snagging extra towels on our way out the door. We send the texts and fill out forms. We show up with extra jackets and make sure everyone has a sandwich; we find an extra pillow to put behind someone's head.

We will get weary. And the weariness is real.

When we run out of steam, we curl up in a ball behind closed doors and cry and eat all the peppermint patties . . . and rally. We recharge. And charge back into the fray. Our girls are there. We have each other via text and DoorDash and phone calls where we cry and rant and tell each other dirty jokes. Like penguins, we drop pebbles at each other's feet . . . Instagram reels and more dirty jokes, recipes and book titles, herbal remedies and methods for getting rid of aphids, empathy and tough love.

To be a woman during these times is to witness resilience, even if emotionally and intellectually, we are stumbled by . . . AGAIN?

No, we will not go back. Already this morning, this morning when I did not want to fall out of bed, badass wild women are reaching out via the tiny personal computer resting beside my notebook and pen. We are a chain of feminine energy crocheted together, holding hands around the globe. We've heard that America is more divided than ever before, but in some ways, that is not true. For during these times, I have drawn closer to those who are in my circle, have come to understand what a true circle can be . . . strong, functional, and hard to break. Hard to crush.

Yesterday morning, while America was at the polls, the globe-trotting surgeon who has worked in war zones unwrapped Gail's finger. The skin graft took; it isn't pretty, but it is pink. He still has the stitches and the wound is still splinted, but the surgeon was pleased. The reality is gruesome, and the pain is real. But we have hope of healing.

I keep thinking about the moment when I saw Gail's pale face and heard his shaky voice. "I did it again."

AGAIN?

"Yeah, and this one is so much worse."

But this time I knew more. This time I knew how to handle the situation, at least a little better. I've got bandages and Bacitracin already in the medicine cabinet. I know how to fill out the forms for workman's comp.

And this election is the same dichotomy. It's so much worse because now we know the shitshow. We've gone swimming in these poisoned waters before. Now we have a name for what happened to the Gospel of Jesus Christ that I grew up with. It has morphed into Christian Nationalism. We know what it is to hear racism and nonsense and lies from the highest office in our nation, from someone who is supposed to be our leader. We know demagoguery.

But we also know how to deal. We know who to trust and who has lost our trust, perhaps forever. We have the readiness to confront this situation rather than just identify it. We have experience with poison and rhetoric. We know where to seek real information and how to turn off the nonsensical noise. We know now to reach out our hands to the hurting and say, "I am here." We know to rest, to save our energy until we know what the battlefield looks like, not respond to all the noise until we know the real threat, know where to do our best work.

Just as being in the emergency room twice in the last few months has caused me to tuck a protein bar in my bag and let it live there, so it has also caused me to be very clear with my people about who I want contacted in case of my own emergency, has given me an appreciation of who will stand by my side so I can better stand to wait in a lobby full of suffering and illness, so I know who will make me laugh with a text and who will give sound advice when I am adrift and bewildered by incoming information, or election results. I know how to treat a crush injury and to explain that we might need an antifungal as well as an antibiotic because of manure and livestock and the dry dirt of drought. I know better how to stand with someone I love in a digital and practical manner, heeding the words of Mr. Rogers: look for the helpers around us and be a helper, too.

Taking snacks to someone in a waiting room is easy. Do it. Listening when someone is hurting and scared is one of the highest forms of love. Give it. Offering a safe place emotionally and/or physically to someone who is disillusioned and marginalized doesn't cost anything. Open your arms.

We are, collectively, tired of life lessons. I hope that Clint doesn't ever have to learn about war through experience, but rather through reading and material presented by good teachers.

It still hasn't rained. I used to say that drought is the most depressing thing I've ever lived through. I was wrong.

But just as I know that it always rains right after a dry spell, so I know that next time Clint brings up war, I will have more, renewed, energy to help him hear the difference between baseball rivalries, presidential elections, and missiles falling on the innocent, leaving so many without homes, horribly wounded, dead.

I have been crushed. But we may find comfort in the knowledge that crush injuries heal. Even if it takes more time than we thought and the pain keeps us up at night . . . even if the wound isn't pleasant to look at and the tissue is numb, we might find a helper along the way who says, "We can do this." We won't ever be the same, but we will join hands in a circle anyway.

And I will pick up my pen and continue to put my yawp on the page.

And, together, we will heal.

THE WILD WILL
ALWAYS WIN

For Tom Hale

As a rule, when a bunch of broncs was needed out of the "stock" horses—there'd be a parada *(herd of about 100 broke horses) held together by a few riders—the wild ones would be hazed (not drove) toward the "parada," the riders holding the milling herd would hide on the sides of their horses and let the wild ones in.*
— Will James, *Cowboys North and South*

"I can't tell you how jealous I am. I would love to be riding with you and Gail. You know, if what you were describing were horses, it would be called a *parada*." I am standing on the porch talking to a dear friend as he lies in a hospital bed, hours to the south. He is ill, and it doesn't look good.

I rode twelve and a half miles, leading Gail's horse while he drove a German military vehicle loaded with gear and hay to this cabin, "Private Property" sign in the window though it sits on the national forest. Tomorrow, we strike out again to the new camp we have established at an alkaline spring in the bottom of a deep rough canyon. I won't have a signal for several days so I call our friend, assure him that even though we will be out of contact, we love him and ask him to please stay alive. After giving me the barest medical details, he asks about the job, about the work. He uses the word *parada*.

Constantly and always fascinated by language, I wrote the word in my journal and began doing research on my phone in that cabin with the windows open and the sound of quail fussing in the underbrush. When I was a little girl, my father told me that *papalote*, the Mexican cowboys' word for windmill, also means *kite*, and *paisano*, the word for the comical roadrunner, also means *countryman*. I am a fish caught on the hook of language and its nuances. But the internet failed me once again and it was only by asking the old cowboys, the old-timers, that I learn that a *parada*, or parade, refers to running a bunch of gentle horses in with a band of wild or feral horses in order to better handle them. The *vaqueros* liked those *broncos* that had been running wild in the desert.

Several weeks ago, we moved a big group of gentle cows to an elevation where everything has stickers and the winters are mild while the summers are brutal and stretch on forever. When I first came to this ranch, we would occasionally see an intrepid dirt biker in all of his protective gear off in there, looking like a color-coded, red-blue green-yellow alien, roaring along, untouched by the terrain, on what were once trails. Sometimes those astride the bikes never saw us at all, sitting on quiet horses in the treeline and bushes waiting for them to pass . . . perhaps because they didn't expect to see us, throwbacks to a time they think is gone. But we are still here while the dirt bike organizations no longer recommend this particular route because it is so rough and so remote. We are still here, riding around in the old way, our saddles, bridles, boots, hats, and even language, anachronistic and adapted to this work that abides even as recreational use of this land comes and goes. Once in a while we see a hunter down there in search of deer or mountain lion—and we speak of him with respect. *He knows what he is doing*, a true outdoorsman on foot rather than putting around on an ATV painted with camouflage colors as if that makes him silent and invisible. I am the only woman I know who rides down there except for all of these grand old mamas, these desert cows, adapted to eating cactus and mesquite beans and catclaw blooms, adapted to thorns and coming to water every other day, or every three. This desert is so female it makes my breasts ache.

Like grown-up relationships, sometimes our work is complicated. Like complicated situations in every line of work, the complication is in the details, so many variables and personalities and circumstances that explanation is exhausting. Why do we have wild cattle in this remote location? So many reasons and years to factor in. But now it is time to clean up the mess, and in order to do so, we have altered our old strategies and established a new camp four miles from the cabin where we normally sleep when we are gathering this piece of the ranch. By doing so, we are saving our horses and ourselves an eight-mile round trip commute in access alone, never mind the rise and fall in elevation. We sleep sixteen miles from ranch headquarters. Gail and a man who has years of experience in catching wild cattle built a set of triggers, or one-way gates, with an "in" and an "out" for the cattle to push through. The "out" can be closed off with a heavy wooden gate when we are ready for these cattle to move uphill to parts of the ranch that are easier to gather. We are using salt blocks and bagged minerals and protein mix as bait.

Until now, I have been a bit disengaged in this project. It all sounded so complicated and a good way for Amy to get yelled at . . . chasing wild cattle in rough country and I'm not good enough. I've seen this little bunch of unbranded feral cattle run before, disappearing in a line over the horizon. The men talk of working them with cow dogs, hold 'em up dogs, while I've been silently vowing to tend camp instead. Quiet quitting out of fear and fatigue. Several weeks ago, I helped move these gentle cows off into this place. By gentle cows, I mean those we see three or four times a year when making a pasture move, the cows that have slept near us at other camps and know our smells and our sounds, that know us as the "hay dudes," that trust us and teach their babies to trust us.

But now, I am sitting on a bay mare in the hot stinkin' desert and we are holding 'em up. Not like a bank robbery, but more like a bending and turning of running creatures back into themselves until they stand and watch us, curious and tired, ready to run again. We hold up the runners with a little group of gentle cows that includes that old white cow and her new calf that looks just like her. She is our Madonna.

"We are training these cows every time they see us." Gail Steiger's sermon, preached every day I've been here, was a huge relief for me, a huge relief from the years I spent with shrinking heart every time the big outfit transient cowboys for hire told stories about some running-off old broad. Their methods and stories often included roping her, tying her down, and pounding Copenhagen in her eyes. Yup, they sure taught her something, alright. But on this ranch, we use number one alfalfa, the promise of our soft "wooo," the sound we make as we throw flakes out in some remote corral, a reward for walking with us. I like cows, and I will always be grateful for these years of getting to know them so well, getting to know their ways of being in the world, the recognition that a cow's whole life is centered on the mother/child relationship. She rises in the cool, nurses her baby, grazes, naps in the shade at water with her friends, grazes back up the slope with the evening sun on her back, beds down with her family group, calf tucked close by her side. Cows are smart, recognizing us and our horses, recognizing, too, when we hire someone new. These mountain desert cows know where the hidden water stays, the best trails, their stomach acid adapting always to available food sources. These smart old mamas teach their babies what is scary and what is not.

The lines are all blurred down here . . . what is wild? The rock squirrel camped out beside the mineral tub in the corrals has never seen a human before. She doesn't know to be scared of me as I walk within a few inches of where she sits in all her fatness, cracking and eating a piñon nut. What is domestic? A maverick bull follows a cow in estrus into the corrals, through the trigger gate. Like the squirrel, he's never, in his five or six years of life, seen a human. In country this rough and remote, it happens all the time. Don't say domestic to this eighteen-hundred pounds of feral muscle and bone. He's been wild since his mama lay down under a mesquite tree and pushed him out into the world. Like the private property cabin that rests on public land, and has for over fifty years, that puzzles these young Forest Service rangers who can't find the rule in their books that makes it legal, so the lines between the domestic and wild are relative. Some things are grandfathered in . . . or grandmothered. The Madonna cow nurses her calf beneath a cedar tree while a maverick bull and a huge old steer we've missed gathering for years watch us, ready to run again. I duck my head and don't look directly at them, no predator stare at those that have gone wild; the mare I'm riding lowers her head to graze, which almost makes us one of the herd.

The old men who would remember the roots of the term *parada* are gone and the men I talk to now keep mentioning some long ago cowboy who used it or refer to having read it in a tattered book in some forgotten line camp. The term is faded and brittle now, the roots strong, a *parade* understandable and standard, but the esoteric *parada* almost gone. At home on my laptop, in some digital archive, I finally find page 38 of *Cowboys North and South* by Will James.

Those times are long gone, the language of *hazed* versus *drove* almost comical, and yet, meaningful to those who handle animals.

But for me, the blending of the wild and the gentle seems a metaphor to hold onto, to snuggle into, to claim as identity and way of being in the world. Something to tattoo on my skin beside the bear tracks inked on the top of my left foot. My whole life has been a *parada*—from the wild that is my father to the sedate domestication that is my mother, from the efforts of a young, naïve woman to break free that resulted in a motorcycle ride in the dark. The driver of the motorcycle, my date, abandoned me at the party and another young man, kind and sober, drove me back to the college campus, but I will always remember that wild ride. I chose the tied-down life of wife and mother on remote ranches where the wild winds blew, reveled in nursing a baby while both of us lay nude in front of the swamp cooler, chose to school my children at home and plant gardens, a life that consumed me until in my mid-thirties the buried spark of creative fire caught and burned down my house. While I am a hearth tender, Hestia at heart, the wildish Artemis in me dances by the fire and I am most at home in places with no doors or walls. Over-domestication of the female causes a fatigue visible in the dairy cows seen from the freeways in our nation, making them appear dumb, and the stench of our own waste is real.

After our *rodear*, our hold-up, less showy rodeo and more time-consuming gentling technique, we turned our horses and rode back to camp. And we did it again the next day, and then the next, long hard days in the saddle and yet each day easier as this wild bunch becomes accustomed to our presence.

We've pulled out of the low country for a few days. Our time is earmarked for meetings in town, a resource monitoring workshop, my granddaughter's last-day-of-school party, restocking the camp box, reshoeing these horses. I have a flare-up of domestication as I water the garden, launder filthy clothing, transpose my handwritten pages to the screen, make phone calls to the men who remember the old ways to ask questions about esoteric words, enjoy a pizza from the oven and ice in my evening drink. When I feel too tethered to my desk, I grab my water bottle and call to the dogs. Midway through our four-mile loop, I tip the bottle to take a drink, startled and then pleased when I remember that the last time I filled it was when we were cutting a big tree that had fallen on the fence down at our new camp. Gail paused and said, "Let's go fill our water bottles in the creek." We walked down to where the water is filled with swimmy things . . . harlequin bugs, a pinch bug with babies crowded on her back, water skimmers, dragonfly larvae, tadpoles . . . and the algae grows in vibrant green puffs. This wild water tastes alive, not like the water we carried there, captive in five-gallon plastic containers. I resume walking only to see a huge bear track in front of me, going right up the graded county road, evidence of the wild right here at home.

"The wild will win." One of the old men I speak to on the phone while I am doing research, seeking a reference for *parada*, warns me that while the concept works in the short term, we shouldn't leave the gentle cows down there too long.

The wild will always win, girl. The wild will always win.

BRING YOUR OWN
BEAUTY

I met the Dog Hater Cow for the first time shortly after I moved onto the ranch. Gail sent me to put out bagged mineral at several dirt tanks up on the mesa. I was new to everything about this place . . . new to the terrain, new to riding a quad on rough trails, new to the vastness of fifty thousand acres. That was before Jim came into our lives and taught me to love dogs. But I did love this man and he had four: Jake, Cooper, Sophie, and Ellie. I wasn't exactly sure where I was going, but I set off anyway, all four dogs running behind.

One of my favorite parts of life is that sometimes, even when we don't quite know where we are going, we might end up somewhere spectacular. When this ranch has had ample moisture, Rincon Tank is both beautiful and peaceful. It rests high up on a mesa in a natural bowl at the foot of Rincon Mountain. The artifacts that litter the ground there are testament to the little valley's enduring attractiveness and life-sustaining attributes.

On that day, I sat on the quad absorbing the moment, so glad I had found the right place, while the dogs cooled bellies and feet in the water. A few cows stood up from their naps in the shade, curious, as I poured the red mineral mix into a metal trough. But the peaceful moment didn't last. I looked up from my task to see a black bald-faced cow with devil horns and a tiny baby that looked just like her running full-on toward me. The threat on her face was real; she meant it. I scurried around to the off side of the quad wondering what in hell was wrong with that cow. She slid to a stop in a cloud of dust and snot, all four dogs now cowering beneath the cooling four-wheeler. This was before we habitually carried cellular phones, but I had a slim digital camera tucked in my shirt pocket. When I got home, I showed Gail her portrait. He said, "Oh, you met the Dog Hater Cow!"

On this morning, years later, I pulled on filthy jeans in a tent up on that same mesa. Day five for these jeans, and I am no longer the new girl around here.

We are using our light camp, stashed here for the duration of this cow works, a one-night camp, second-string gear, corned beef hash, canned chili with beans, Spam, and oatmeal packets. I've recently discovered envelopes of precooked rice/quinoa blend, add two table-spoons of water, heat in a saucepan over the fire. They help vary the menu when we get here at dusk with cows, no matter that my husband is skeptical about cowboys eating quinoa.

It is over twelve miles from the cabin in the low country to ranch headquarters, so as we dig the cows out of the hidden pockets in the desert, we move them in two stages, sleeping here in this water lot overnight before going on.

It is five a.m., and I can hear Gail building the fire on last night's ashes. Just as the tiniest sip of whiskey rests in the bottom of my tin cup as I dress by headlamp, so the conversation from last night lingers. In the love letters I've penned, I've left out the reality of two strong-willed people, both stubborn enough to ride out here and do this job, both vocal and fiercely protective of our own inner territory. I've left out our clashes.

These fifteen-plus years have proved Gail's early assertion that if we can work cows together, we can do anything together, but yesterday we had a huge fight, right in the middle of the cow drive, fueled by frustration and fatigue. We both consider the best defense to be a good offense, so words were said, fingers were pointed, and wounds were reopened, at high volume. An old story in the kingdom of coupledom. Imagine compounding the situation with working together always and no showers and no spaces in our togetherness. We couldn't find a way back to our peace until the Dog Hater Cow, now old enough to vote, lay down in the middle of the trail. She was hot and thought we were yelling at her. She decided she'd walked far enough and sank to the ground, her big bull calf standing dutifully by her side.

Nothing breaks up a marital spat as effectively as the ridiculous.

We got that old cow up twice, but the third time she lay down, we had no choice but to move the rest of the cows around her and go on. She trailed us up, as we knew she would, caught up with us by the time we reached water. She spent the night bedded down under the tree next to our tent, the calves in this group a constellation sleeping around her.

But in the dusk, after we unsaddled, I was still aching from the fight, still aching to fight. I pulled my chair from the pile of camp stuff, built a fire, and sat down. Hell was going to freeze over before I cooked a goddamned thing. I'd eat gingersnaps and drink whiskey.

One of the good things about no spaces in our togetherness is that, as so many couples who had to shelter in place now know, we have to face up. We have nowhere to run when we must crawl into the same tent or under the same bedroll tarp. In the conversation around the fire, after he heated a can of chili and one of those quinoa packets, it ceased to matter what the fight had actually been about. We found our way to listing the things we have learned in the last several years. While my own accounting may look a bit different than his, I have learned that it damn sure matters being married to someone who, at five a.m., in a tent full of dirt in the wilderness, says something like, "Now move over, little spider. Don't you bite anyone." Sound of the tent zipper. "You move on out of here."

And now, as the cows chew hay and the sky begins to lighten and the fire begins to crumble into bright red coals, I pull my journal from my saddle bag and write my list, starting with that conversation with the spider.

I have learned to face the rock, not the fall. To trust in gravity and the toeholds and the handholds, to lean in to the hard things. More than anything I have learned to trust my horse and her footing in these rocks. Perhaps I am learning, also, to trust myself.

I have learned that at its very best, life is work, and meaningful work enhances our lives in beautiful ways. I have discovered that I love my lifework and how one type of work can feed another and that no matter how much money I may or may not have, I will show up to the work because that means showing up to me.

I have learned that the most important religion is "do no harm." I believe in carrying the crickets outside rather than flushing them down the toilet. I don't believe in crushing another's song.

I have learned that when I am out here, fear subsides into the sand and the creekbank and the strong roots and the fragile brilliant wings. I have learned to pause in the places of beauty and take pictures of cool caterpillars, even if I have to hold my bridle reins in my teeth to do so.

Nylon ropes have taught me that sometimes I hold on too tight and that throwing it all away might be better than getting burned down to the bone, an applicable lesson in so many situations.

A man named David taught me to eat the best meals first. He said that when we stop to make camp, drop our packs for the night, dig into the stash of dehydrated meals we brought along, we should choose the one we like best. That way, the next night, we can do the same thing. And so on, through the whole journey. It is pretty good advice since we never know when the journey will be over and we won't have the opportunity to pick between teriyaki chicken and Italian sausage pasta ever again.

The isolation of this life, magnified by a pandemic, has taught me that it matters who peoples our world, both in our physical space and on the screen. Some may come along simply to show us and themselves and the world that they can endure, that they are tough. These people might or might not relax their competitive natures and see the seep monkeyflower with its tiny face, appreciate the hummingbird moments. And it is okay to say no, to ride out alone, rather than be responsible for someone else's emotions when the sun beats down and the rocks go on forever. Intentional solitude is where we meet ourselves, head-on, which is probably one of the scariest things a human being will ever do. Do it anyway. We may stop chasing the constant crowd, the constant companionship, and become our own best lovers.

When I am in the wilderness, alone, I see that I am never alone. She shows me that I am not very important. And then tells me that I am.

I have learned to embrace silence. Silence can be as scary as solitude for some people who listen to constant noise. Turn off the music, the podcast, the incessant news feed, the candy-coated entertainment, and listen to what is being said in your own depths, the birdsong of your own wisdom.

We are not obligated to show people our hearts, our special places, that which is sacred to us. Sometimes we love what we love, believe what we believe, and it is okay not to drag everyone along with us. And when someone special shows up, someone who gets it, someone who will help shake the dirt out of the bedroll after an exhausting day, someone who will flank up without being asked, someone who gently moves a spider out of the tent before dawn, don't take them for granted because those people are rare.

I believe it is okay to be cranky at night when you've worked hard all day. Forgive yourself the doubt and bad decisions. Stretch your tired muscles and rest. And then forgive your partner when they are just as cranky. Forgive everyone their missteps just as you ask forgiveness for your own.

I believe in reading books, hard books, books that make us think. It is one of my joys in life to watch my guy read a good book that I have already read, watching it like a movie playing across his face.

I believe in bathing less, in moving my body more, in growing some of my own food, in clean dirt, in eating as close to the source as possible, in sleeping and swimming nude. I believe in sweat and woodsmoke and breastmilk and metamorphosis as metaphor—what are you becoming?—and sleeping on the ground. I believe in feeding the birds and coming to each relationship as a complete human, but also in leaving pieces of ourselves behind, like the shedding of old tired skin.

I have learned to make mornings and evenings sweet, bookending my days with peace and ritual rather than screens and input.

This place has the magic cure. It shows me where the wild things live and shows me that I am one of them. I go out there to lose the dried-up scales of over-domestication. I must work to get out there, to where we are all wild, leaving tracks on the verges of damp and scat in the dirt behind the rock.

Out there I am a nest-builder and a song-singer. I embrace the ritual of fire and the precious beauty of water. I was twin sisters in ancient times . . . Artemis with her bow drawn, barefoot, fierce, awake, and Hestia with her sacred sanctuary. In this modern world I have the magic and know the potion. I know where the wild lives and am at home in this world.

I believe in words until they fade to hum. I believe in sunrise even on a cloudy day. I believe that evil exists. Negative energy exists, and it matters not what name we give it. Sometimes it comes bearing wisdom. We are feeling our way through together, trying not to step on each other's toes, spelunking through the dark caves of life. Bullets fly. Rape is real. Sickness within the core of humanity spreads like a fungus, and it always has, just as each of us carries our own cancer cells. Blood has been shed, and it can rob us of our peace, like a thief that robs us of our gold or our identity. For a time, we sit bereft, in a pool of humanity's spilled lifeblood. We mourn, and we tear our hair, and we ask questions in keening voices, and we lash out with, "How could this happen and who do we blame?"

I am not sure I believe in the empirical, the irrefutable, and I have defied both gravity and lift. Call me naïve.

The earthquakes come and I choose them because I choose here and now, not the same as control. I choose again the joy, and the fear and the grief that are the necessary shadows of loving, and the drudgery that is the shadow side of giving back because, heaven knows, others have given to me. I have learned that someday I might be big enough to embrace it all, embrace this love, this living, this being, this spin. It is dark, light, drought, flood, arctic cold and Sahara heat, sting and flow and danger and bite and safety and rage and soothe and husk and kernel and wing and burrow and harsh and gentle and the sun comes up and goes down and the moon shows her full face or her fuck-you fingernail.

The choice is ours—and we choose to be here.

Today is the perfect day to smile and to dance, not in celebration, but in defiance of that which would rob us of our peace. Today is the perfect day to lie with the one you love and feel fully human and alive. Perhaps tears will leak onto the pillow. Perhaps they should.

Today is the perfect day for ice cream or a scrambled egg sandwich with extra mayo. And pickles. We might see a pair of pelicans floating in the water held by a dirt dam on a mesa in the high desert. It is true. We might. Today is perfect because it dawned.

I have learned that there is a party going on. We recognize that celebration in spring with the effusive blooming after a good rain. We see the glorification of the rightful cycle in autumn, reminding us that the decline to entropy is necessary so that the seeds may rise again for they don't truly die—the perfect illustration of reincarnation.

This glorious party is continued in the ants' busyness and building, in the birds' swoop and dance, in the soft pad of feet in the night—for isn't every journey or feast an opportunity to celebrate?

And sometimes, even when we are not quite sure where we are going, we end up somewhere spectacular.

Bring your own beauty.

ACKNOWLEDGMENTS

I am a connoisseur of acknowledgment pages. I never skip them.

While I have written my own for previous books, I acknowledge that what I need, and who I look to for support, shifts and changes with the years.

First and foremost, this time around, I want to thank the circle of other dedicated writers who have persevered around me, up close and personal and daily . . . Elliott Cox, Juni Fisher, Barbara Newman, Evelyn Roper, and Jamie McDonald. You are my constant, the river within the ocean, and we carry each other along.

To those I have watched from afar . . . David James Duncan, Kat Wilder, Susan Tweit, Andy Wilkinson, Sean Sexton, and Forrest VanTuyl . . . thank you for inspiring me to reach higher and higher.

To members of the daily prompt group that have ebbed and flowed through the years, I owe a great debt. Because you keep showing up, six sentences at a time, so must I. Rabbit, rabbit.

The big gap of years between the publication of this book and the one previous means that this one has undergone many iterations. Sandra Bishop read every single one, believed in me even though she knew I would break her heart. This book exists in this form and with this title because of her. Sandra, we told them so.

To JR at FSG, together we thumb our noses at marketing committees. What do they know? Thanks for trying.

To the team at TTUP, especially Travis Snyder, thank you for, once again, taking a chance on me.

Thank you to all the coffee shops and bars and cafés that have put up with me and the laptop for hours at a time. Even though I live in "a cabin in the woods," a change of scenery always helps.

The writing is one thing; the living is another. Without my days lived here on the land, here in this wild and precious place, I would have nothing to write about. My deepest gratitude to Gail Steiger, Saint Randy, Tom Polk, Jim, Bella, Linda, Birdie, BB, Ike, and Maddie. To a little cow named Flo and an old bull we called Big Red.

To my Witches. Circles are hard to crush.

I extend a heart full of gratitude to Dr. Cari Babitzke for giving me Boston, for a friendship I have always longed for, for helping put into words concepts my brain and heart already know. For blazer shopping in thrift stores and lobsters in the rain. For ice cream on the beach.

Thank you to Brooksie for that first white enamelware mug.

To Shellie Derouen for numerous videotapes of *Friends*, all those years ago.

To my waffle friends . . . Stephanie, Jessica, Shellie, Elliott, and Jamie. Your support and friendship are invaluable.

Being a Mamie for the last ten years has been one of the best parts of life. Clint Lucas and Kamber Ann . . . may you always love coming to the Spider to hang out with me and Grampa Gail.

On the living side of things, no one has taught me more than those humans I grew under my heart. Oscar, you are perfectly imperfect and stronger than you know. Thank you for sending me pictures of roadrunner nests and calling me to unravel knotty thoughts. Diamonds would mean less.

Lily, I have reserved this spot for you on purpose. It is an honor to do life with you, to be in a position to witness your bravery and resilience. Thank you for showing the way up and out and through, and for the best playlists ever. Not only are you one of my favorite people to hang out with, but you are wise and discerning. I'd hike, run rapids, read, and travel with you, any day, and that is saying a lot.

ABOUT THE AUTHOR

Amy M. Hale is the author of *Ordinary Skin* and *Rightful Place*, the 2012 WILLA winner for creative nonfiction and Foreword Reviews Book of the Year for essays. She is also the author of *Winter of Beauty* and *The Story Is the Thing*. Hale cowboys for Spider Ranch in Yavapai County, Arizona, and performs poetry, speaking to groups all over the country.

AUTHOR PHOTO BY JESSICA BRANDI LIFLAND